Quick & Easy Accordion Book: Tex Mex Edition
Published by F-flat Books, Philadelphia, PA

ISBN: 978-1-63991-163-9

About the book

The Quick and Easy Accordion Book introduces **beginners** to the fundamentals of **playing the accordion** through a straightforward and accessible method. The **primary focus** is on **learning the G major scale** by playing each note individually and practicing exercises designed to develop finger agility through varied sequences. In addition to scale work, this **method reinforces essential techniques** such as **proper bellows control** and gradually builds arm and finger strength and endurance. This modern instructional approach has been successfully used with beginning students for many years, consistently producing excellent results in helping learners start playing confidently and progress rapidly.

This book serves as an introduction to:

- Learning the parts of the accordion
- Practicing exercises in the **G scale** to build foundational skills
- Playing along with high-quality Conjunto music tracks to better understand the genre and focus on playing on the beat.
- Identifying button shapes used for proper fingering in accordion scales
- Learning to play basic chords: G Major, D Major, E minor, and C Major

I'm thrilled to welcome you to the world of **Diatonic Accordion** and wish you all the best as you **begin your journey** with this **unique and exciting instrument and musical style.**

About the book

This book is designed for those eager to learn how to play the diatonic accordion in the **Tex-Mex/Conjunto style**. This vibrant musical tradition, also known as Conjunto music, originated in South Texas and blends the lively rhythms of German polka with unique regional flair. Often credited to pioneering accordionist **Narciso Martínez** of San Benito, TX, Conjunto music has grown into a rich and essential part of Tejano and Mexican-American culture.

The **accordion** is a self-accompanying instrument, much like the piano. The **right hand plays the melody** using the treble buttons, while the **left hand provides rhythm and harmony** with the bass buttons.

In modern Conjunto music, accordion players typically focus on playing the **melody with their right hand using the treble buttons**, while the **left hand is mainly used** to press the bass buttons to **control air flow**—similar to using an air valve. In this style, the traditional role of the **bass buttons** has been largely **replaced by the Bajo Sexto**, a 12-string Mexican guitar that provides rhythm and harmony. This shift allows accordionists to concentrate on performing more complex and expressive melodies.

Table of Contents

Table of Contents

Table of Contents

Brief History of the Accordion

The **diatonic button accordion** is a cornerstone of Tex-Mex/Conjunto music, a genre that emerged in South Texas during the late 19th and early 20th centuries. German and Czech immigrants introduced the accordion to **Texas and northern Mexico,** where it was embraced by Mexican-American and Tejano musicians. Early Conjunto pioneers like **Narciso Martínez** adapted the **button accordion** to traditional Mexican folk music, pairing it with the **bajo sexto,** a 12-string guitar, to craft the distinct **Conjunto sound**. Over time, influential artists such as **Valerio Longoria, Tony De La Rosa,** and **Flaco Jiménez** helped modernize the genre by incorporating new rhythms, instruments, and cross-genre influences. Today, the accordion remains at the heart of Conjunto music—both as a symbol of cultural identity and as a vibrant, evolving instrument for new generations of musicians.

Purchasing the Right Accordion

There are many great accordion brands for beginners and professionals alike. I recommend the Hohner Panther for beginners, though other good options are available. When buying a diatonic accordion, **remember it's tuned to a specific key**—like a harmonica—so while the fingering stays the same across keys, the pitch will vary.

Here are the common keys that diatonic accordions come in:

- * G Accordion- **(GCF) SOL**
- F Accordion- **(FEbBb) FA**
- E Accordion- **(EAD) MI**
- **This BOOK IS FOR G ACCORDION (GCF)**
    - ***Note:*** *To play along with others using this book, all accordion players should use instruments tuned to the same key.*

If you're purchasing a used accordion, be sure to:

- Check for air leaks: The accordion should not open or close on its own without pressing a key or button. Uncontrolled movement could indicate internal damage.
- Confirm the tuning: Ensure the accordion is tuned to the key you need for your playing or ensemble use.
- Test all buttons and keys: Press each one to make sure it produces a clear sound and functions properly.

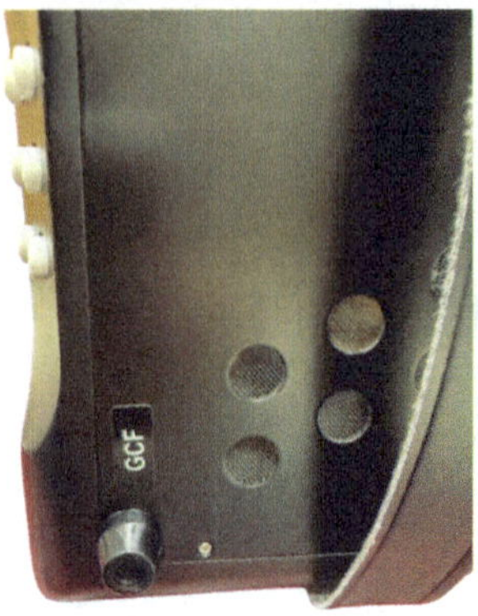

34 buttons vs. 31 buttons

The two most common accordion brands in conjunto music are the Italian-made **Gabbanelli** and the German-made **Hohner.**

Both are played the same way, but one has 3 additional keys. **Gabbanelli and similar accordions have 34 buttons, while Hohner and similar accordions have 31 buttons**.

In this book, we provide a **31-button chart**, but if you have a **34-button accordion, you can still use the same chart**. The only difference is that 34-button accordions have **three extra buttons at the bottom of the treble board**, which produce three higher notes. If you're using a **34-button accordion**, simply **ignore those three extra notes** while following the chart.

3 extra keys

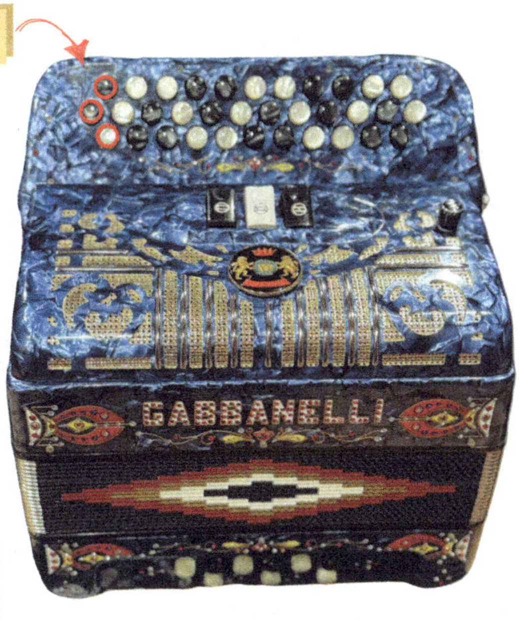

34 Buttons

31 Buttons

Instrument Care

Accordions are delicate instruments, as they are made of wood and contain reeds inside the box, held in place by **wax**.

Because of this, **NEVER** leave an accordion in hot environments, such as a car or garage, as the heat can melt the wax and damage the interior of the instrument.

Also, never try to close the bellows with force. Always use the **air valve button** to release the air inside the accordion. The accordion functions like a balloon and needs to be sealed properly. If the bellows are damaged, air will escape, creating a leak that makes it much more difficult to play.

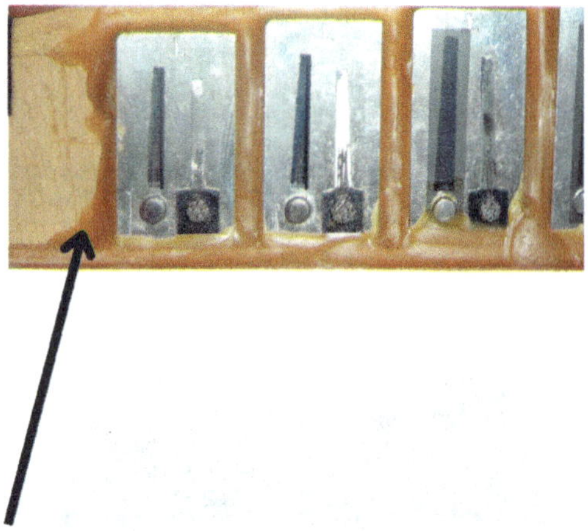

WAX

Placing the Accordion Down

When setting the **accordion down, always use the feet at the bottom of the instrument.** Placing it on its side can cause damage to the bellows over time.

If the accordion **is open when placing it down, avoid pushing it closed with force**. Instead, gently close the bellow and **secure the top bellows strap before setting it down.** I also recommend **placing it on the floor rather than on a chair** to prevent accidental falls.

Accordion foot

Parts of the Accordion

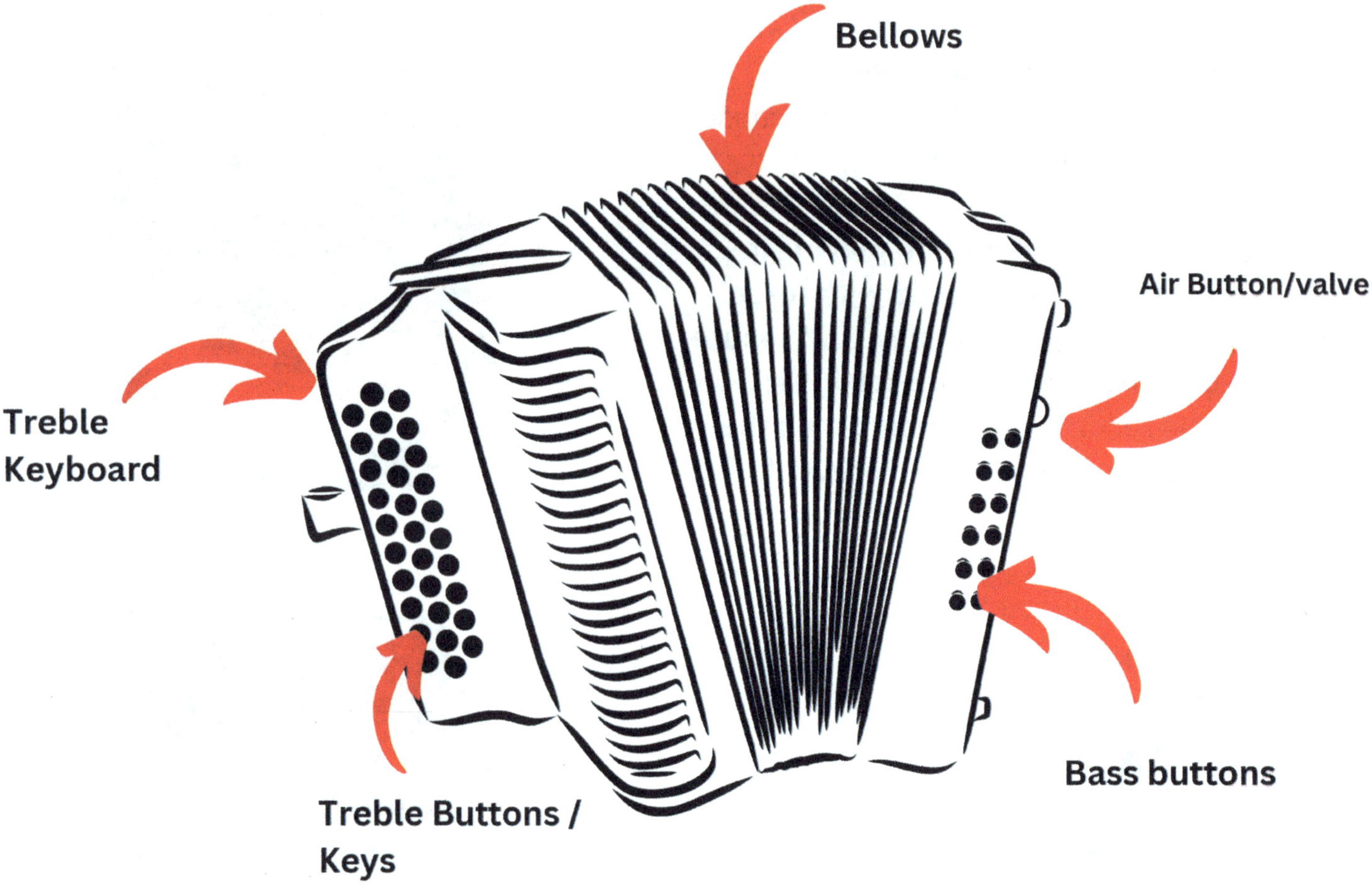

How to Hold an Accordion

STEP 1
Sit up straight and place the accordion sideways on your lap, with the treble buttons facing your right side.

STEP 2
Adjust the shoulder straps so that the accordion stays at the same height when you stand and sit. Test this by standing up and sitting down to ensure consistent positioning.

STEP 3
Rest your right thumb along the edge of the treble board, with your fingers hovering comfortably over the treble buttons.

STEP 4
Insert your left hand into the bass strap, with your thumb positioned near the air valve button.

Bass Strap

Playing our first notes

Playing an accordion can be confusing because **each button has two different notes.** When pushing a button and **pulling the bellows out**, you will **get one note** and pushing the same button and **pushing the bellows in** will get you a **different note**.

This can be confusing at first, so we'll begin by **focusing only on the notes played while pulling the bellows out**.

In this book, we will **concentrate** on the **G scale**, using **only** the **right hand** on the **treble buttons**. This approach will help build a strong foundation before introducing notes with bellows in.

Only
Bellows out

Treble Buttons

Low and High Pitches

On the accordion, the **top buttons** in each row generally produce the **lower-pitched notes**, while the **bottom buttons** produce the **higher-pitched notes**. However, the **very top button in each row** is an exception—these are called **accidentals**, and they don't follow the standard note pattern.

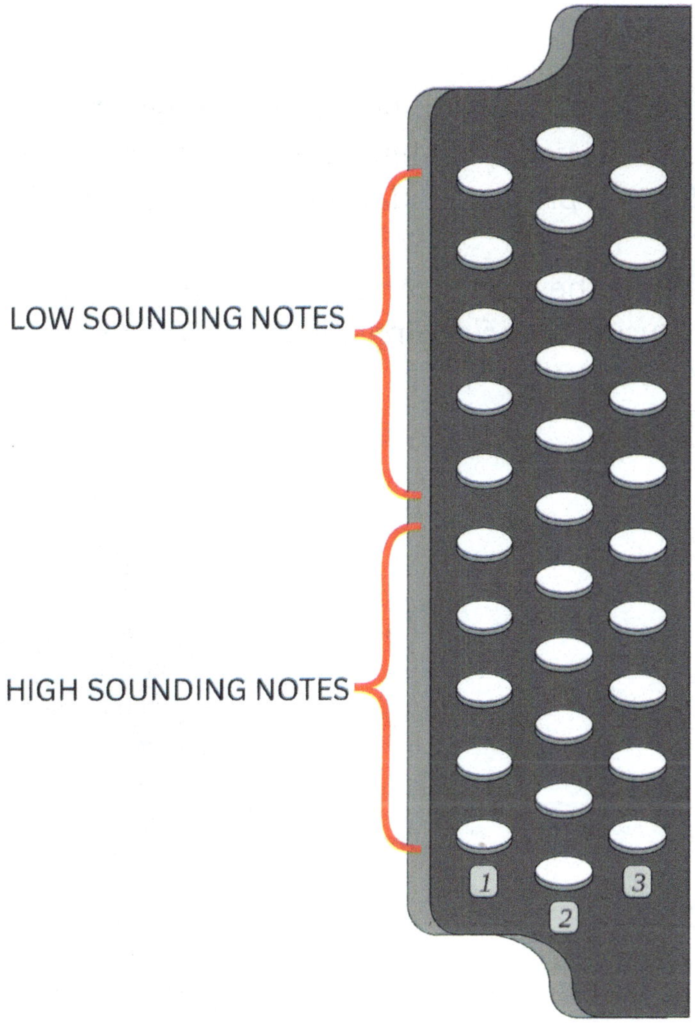

Right Hand Position

Rest your right-hand thumb along the edge of the treble board. Practice keeping your thumb in this position while using your other fingers to press the buttons. This will help develop proper hand positioning and control.

Note: While the thumb can be used to press buttons at more advanced levels, we will start by using only four fingers—index, middle, ring, and pinky.

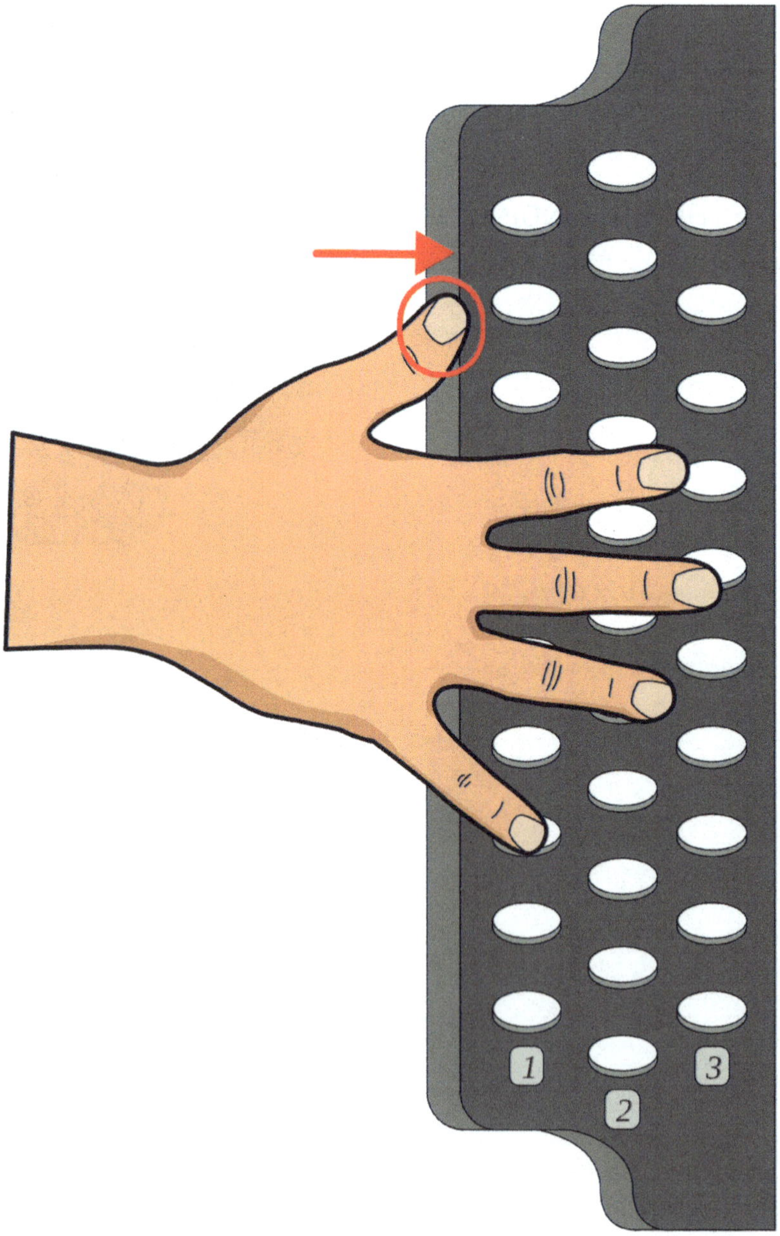

Finger Names

We will label each finger using its initial letter. While finger placement may vary depending on the notes or buttons being played, it's important to choose the most efficient fingering for each pattern. In this book, you will have a suggested fingering to play each exercise. We will primarily focus on using the index, middle, and ring fingers. However, the use of the pinky is encouraged as you progress.

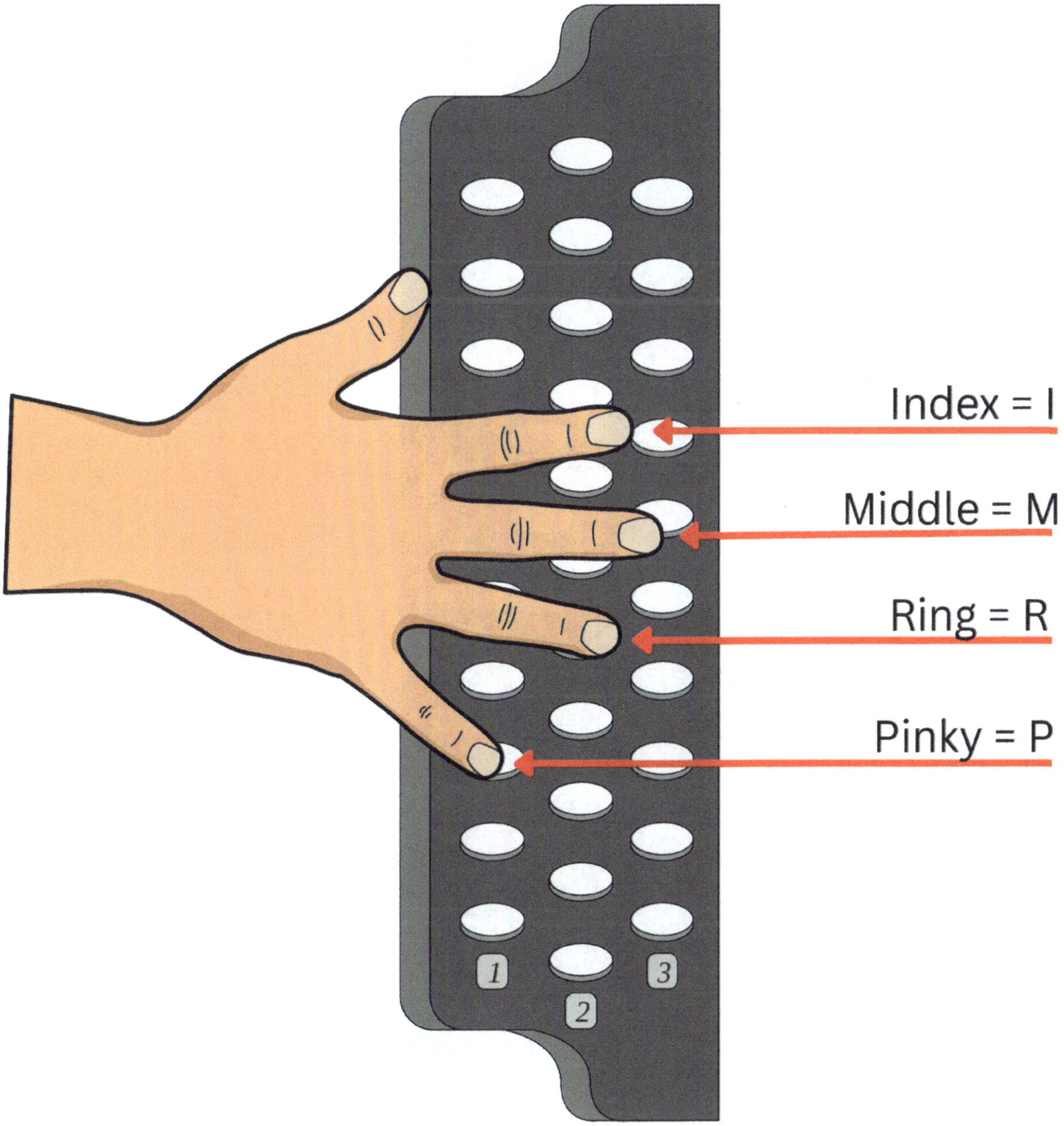

The Accordion Rows

Let's take a look at the **treble board**. The diatonic accordion has **three vertical rows**. Memorizing these three rows will make it **easier** to **locate the notes**.

Visualizing the treble board this way will help you **find** the **notes faster** and **develop muscle memory** for the shapes and order of the scales.

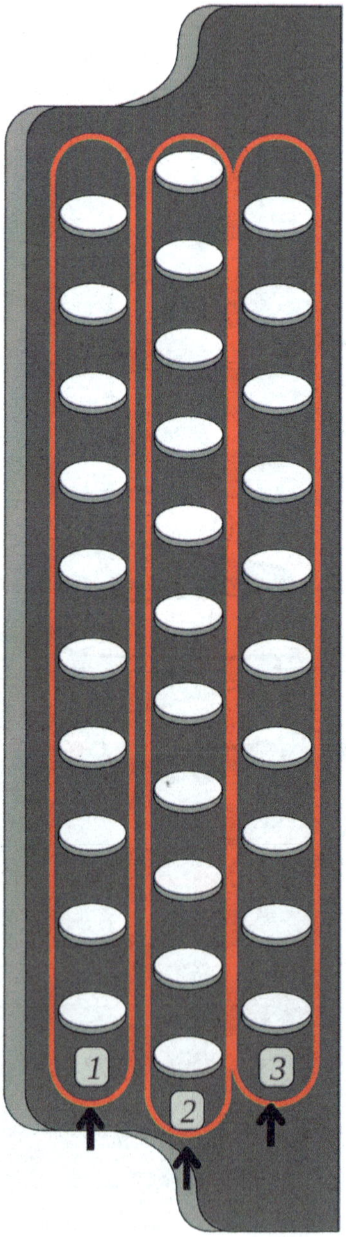

Learning G

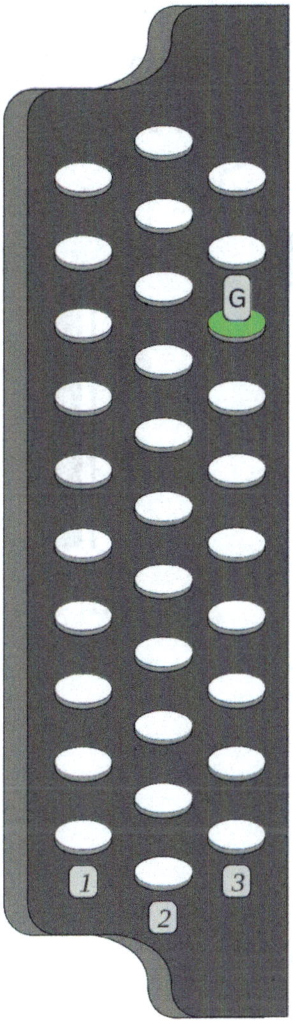

Suggested Fingering

G = Index

Learning A

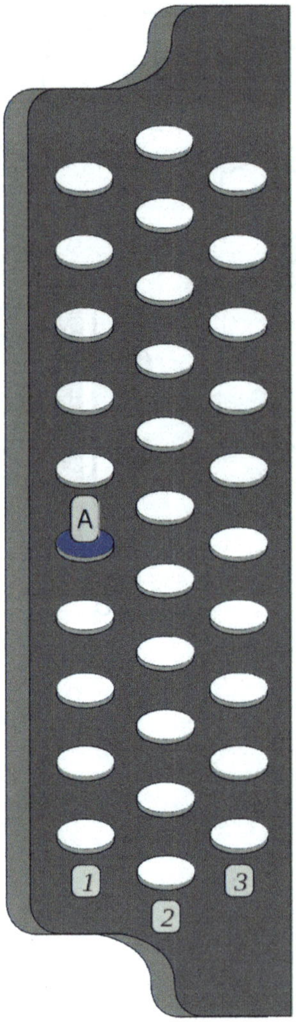

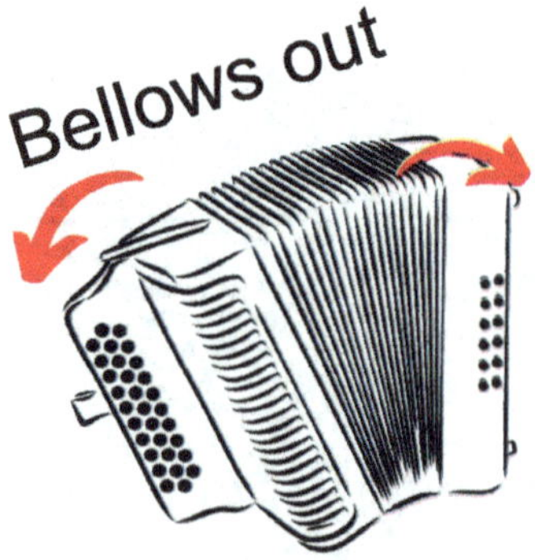

Suggested Fingering

A=Ring

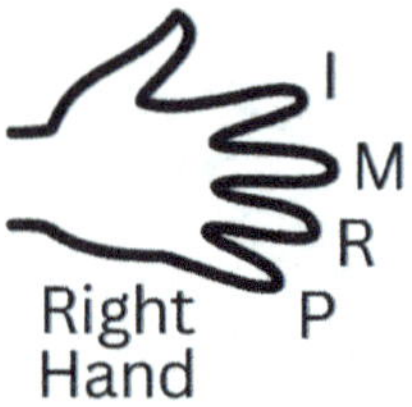

Learning B

Suggested Fingering

B = Middle

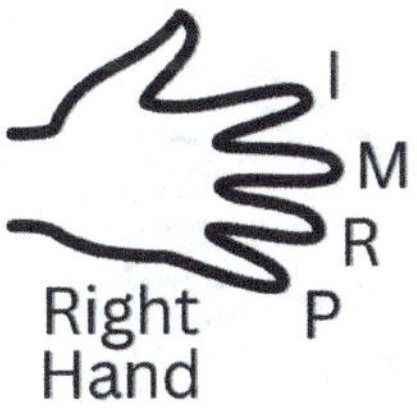

Polka #1

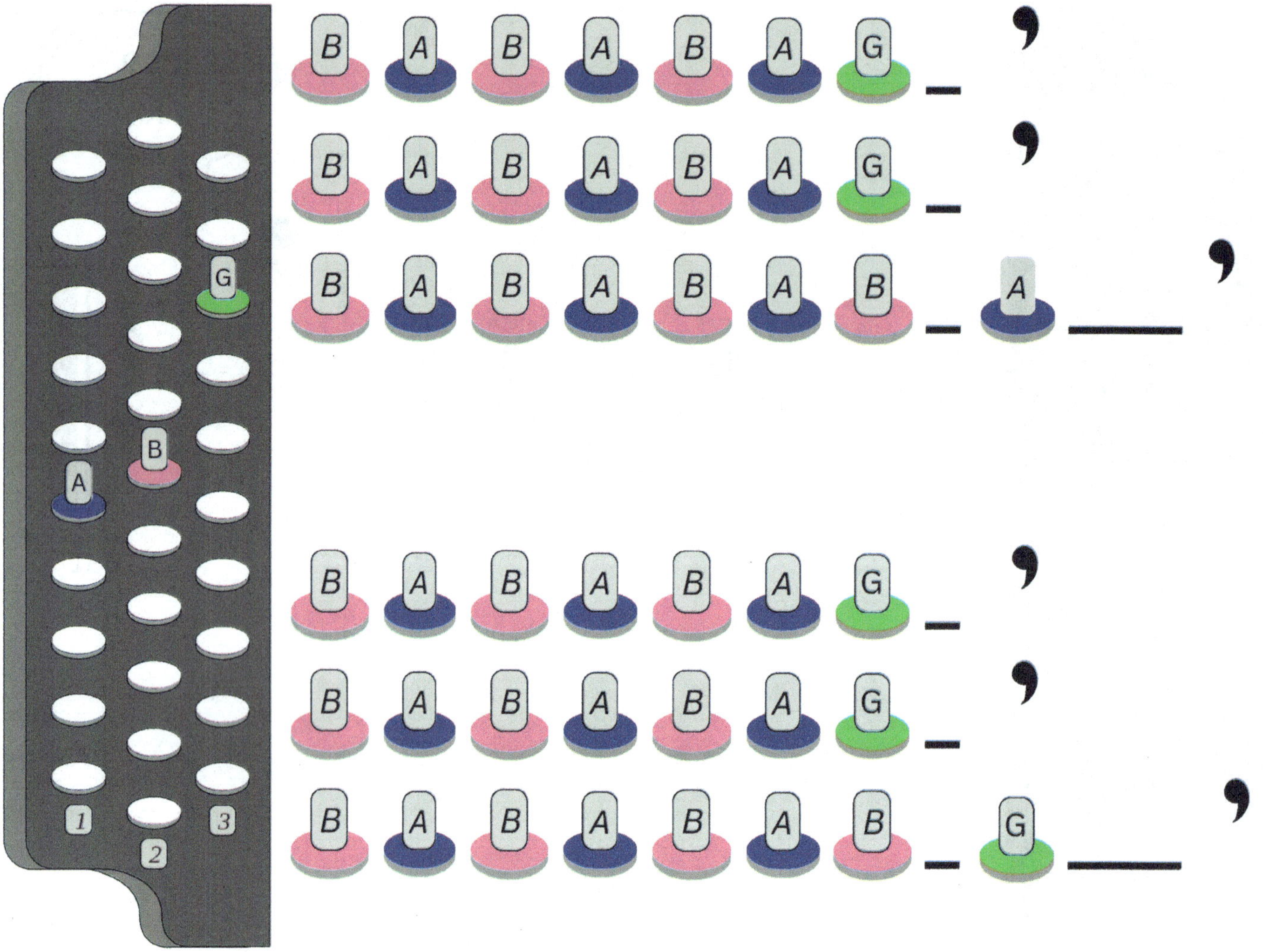

Suggested Fingering

G = Index

A = Ring

B = Middle

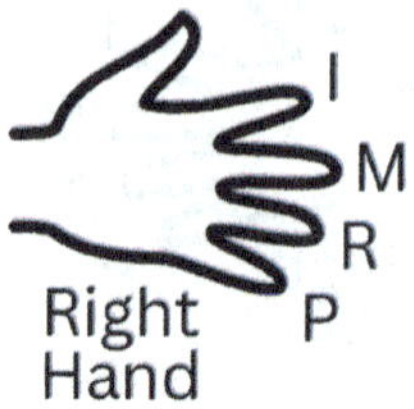

Polka #2

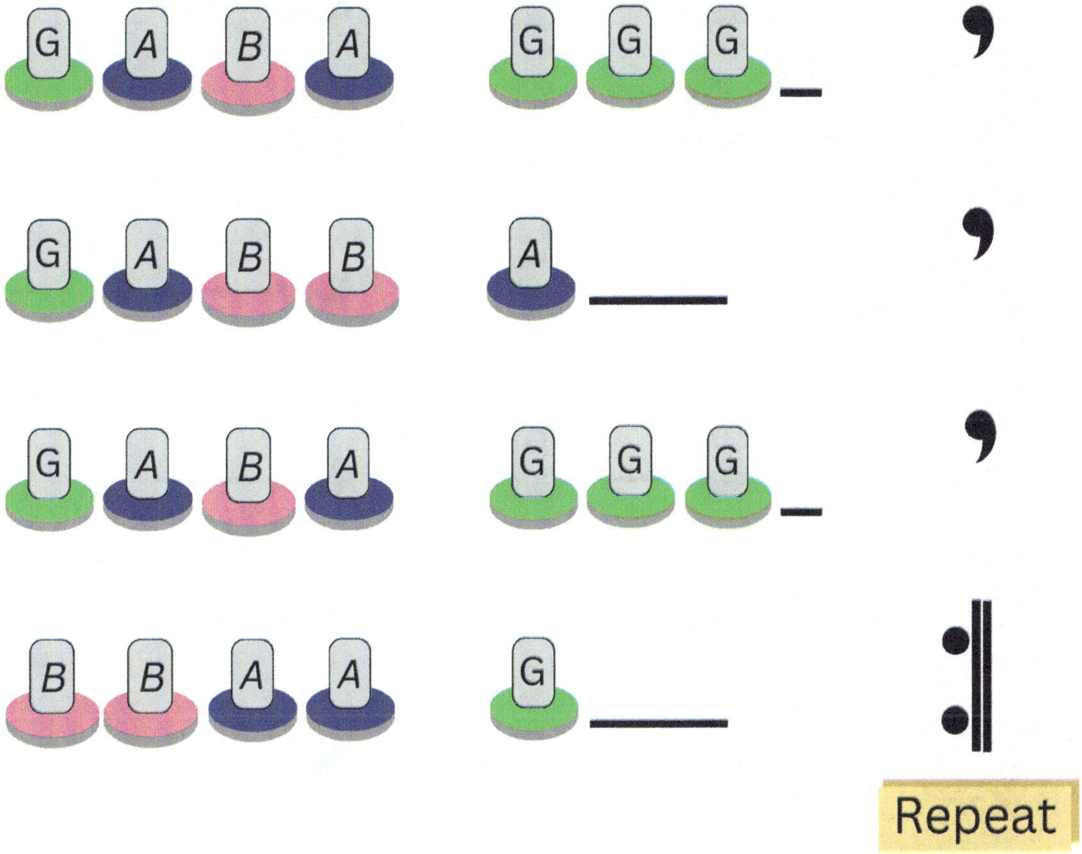

Suggested Fingering

G = Index
A = Ring
B = Middle

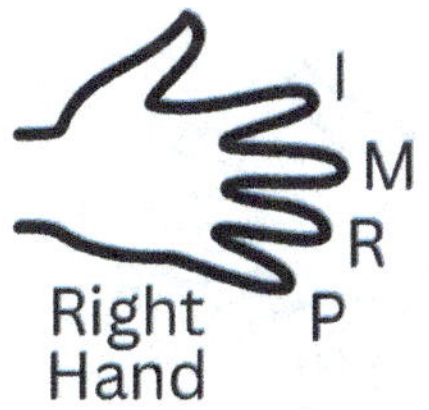

Cumbia #1

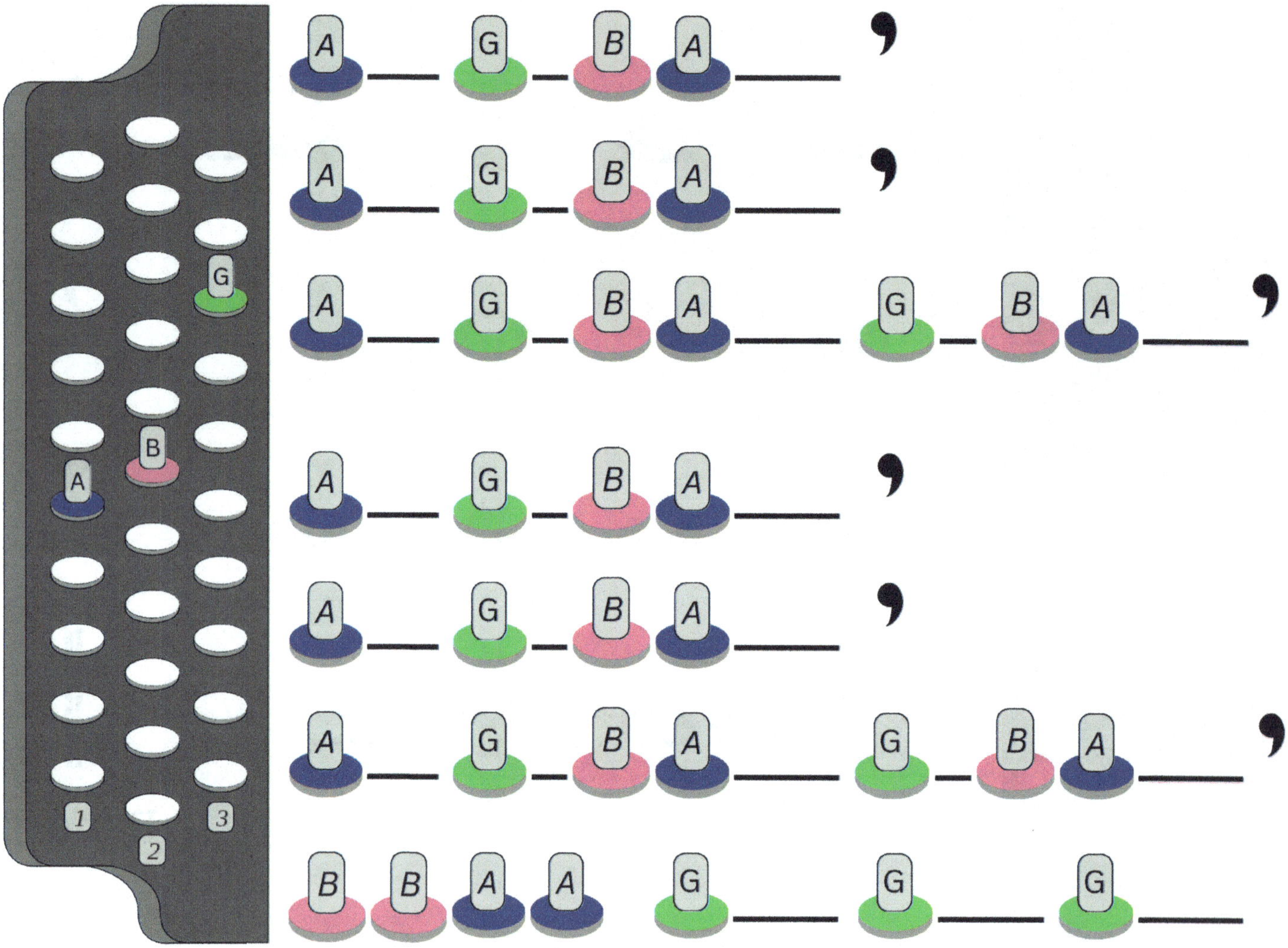

Suggested Fingering

G = Index
A = Ring
B = Middle

Cumbia #2

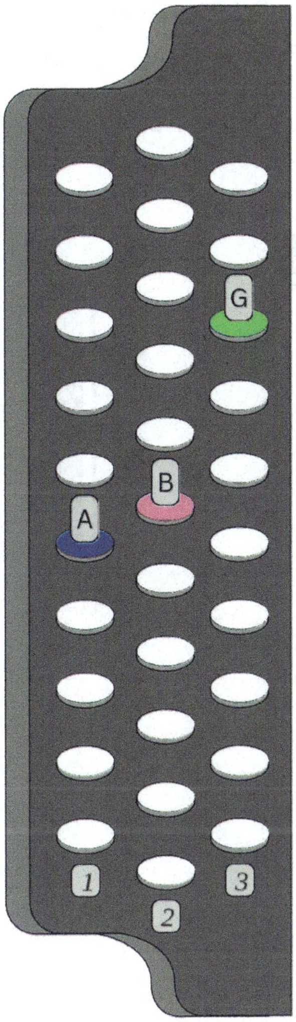

G B G B G ——— G ,

G B G B A ——— A ,

A B A B A ——— A ,

A B A B G ——— G ,

G B G B G ——— G ,

G B G B A ——— A ,

A B A B A ——— A ,

A B A B G ——— G ,

Suggested Fingering

G = Index

A = Ring

B = Middle

Learning C

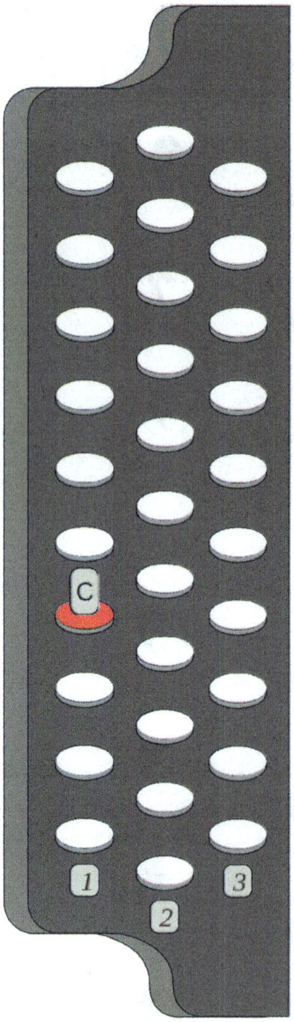

Suggested Fingering

C = Ring

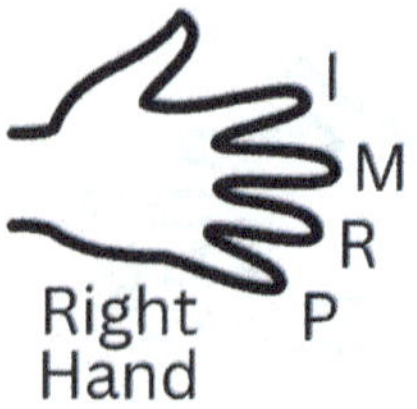

Learning D

Suggested Fingering

D = Middle

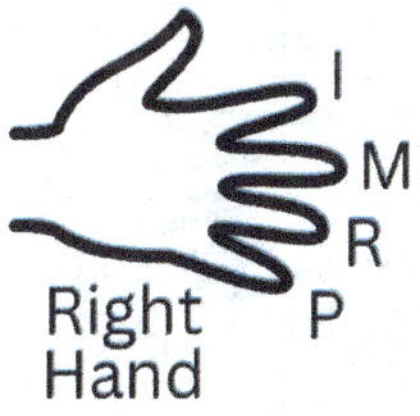

G Major - 5 notes

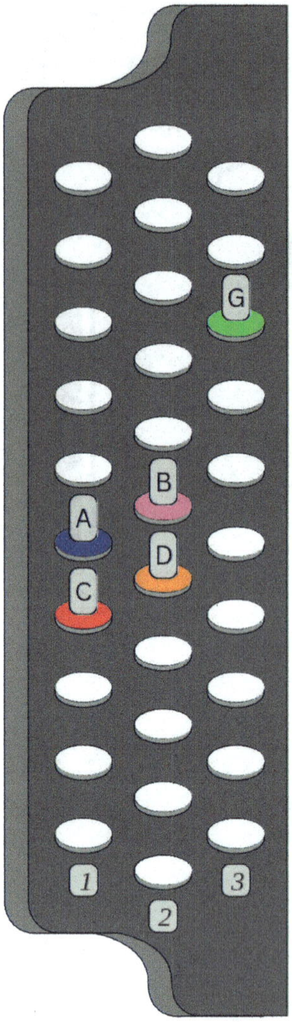

Suggested Fingering

G = Index
A= Ring
B= Middle
C= Ring
D= Middle

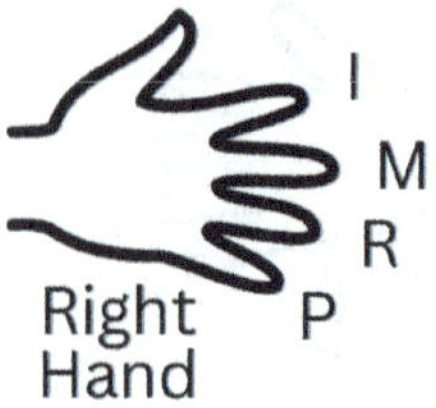

Cumbia #3

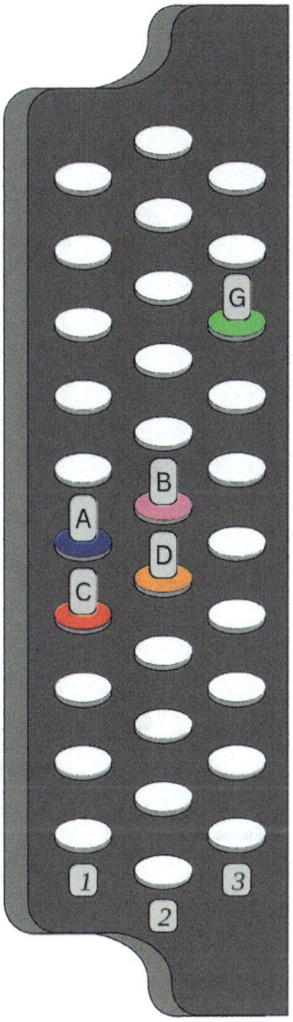

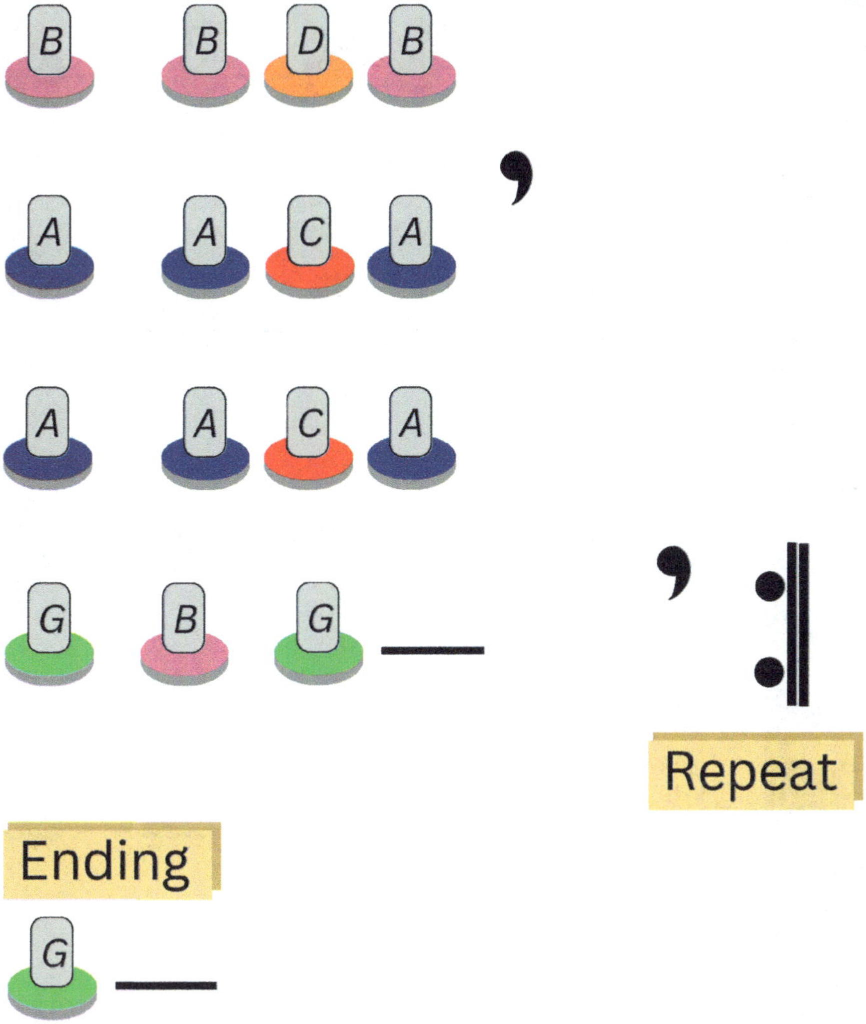

Suggested Fingering

G=Index
A=Middle
B=Middle
C=Ring
D=Ring

Polka #3

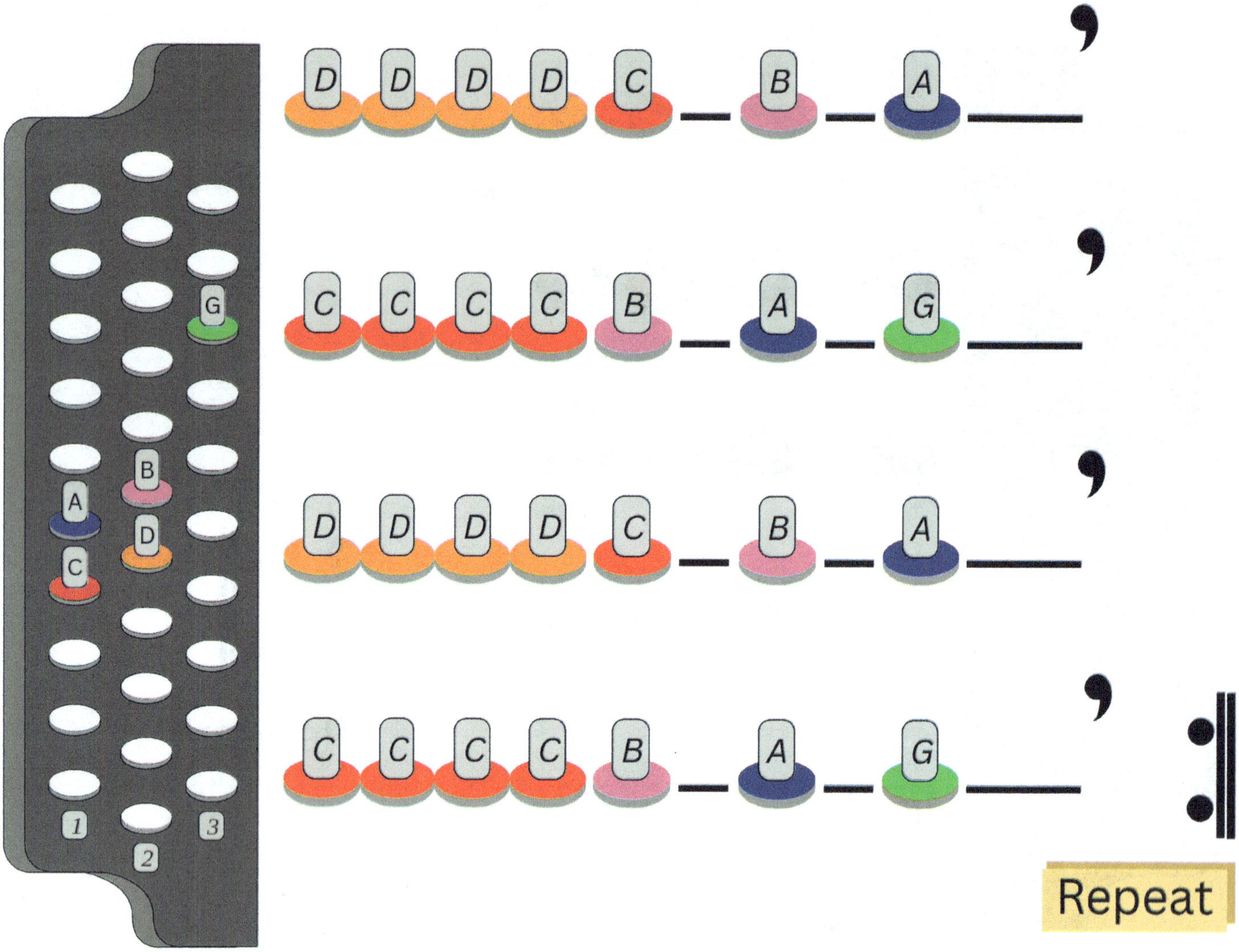

Suggested Fingering

G=Index
A=Middle
B=Index
C=Middle
D=Index

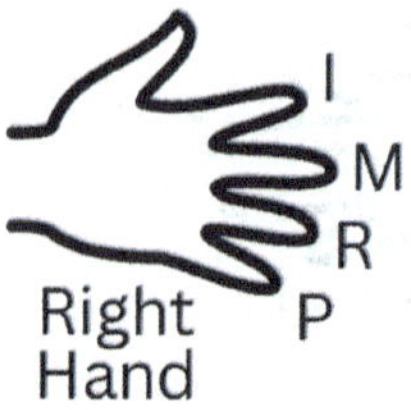

Polka #4

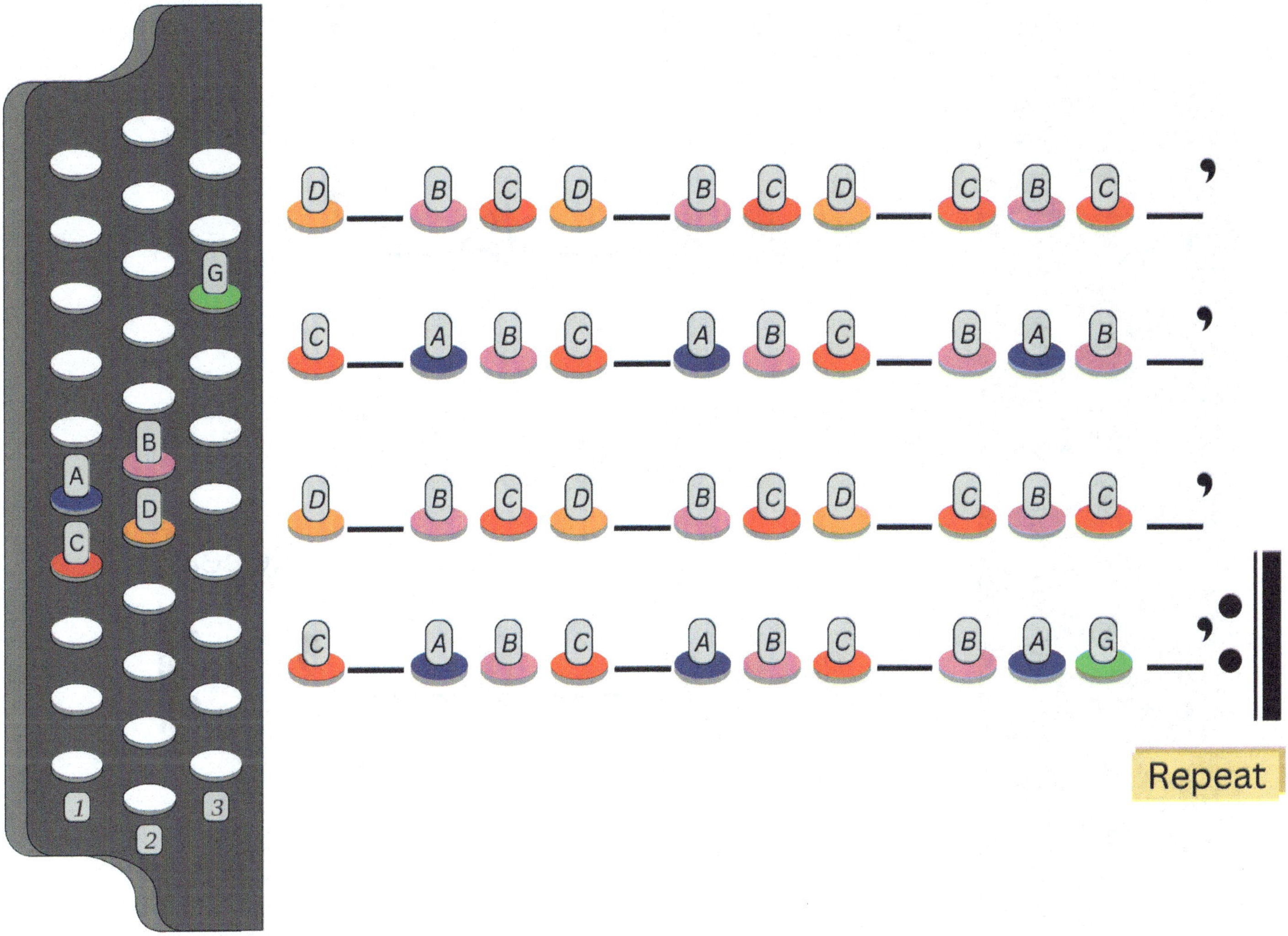

Suggested Fingering

G=Index

A=Middle

B=Index

C=Middle

D=Index

Tao Tao Beginner

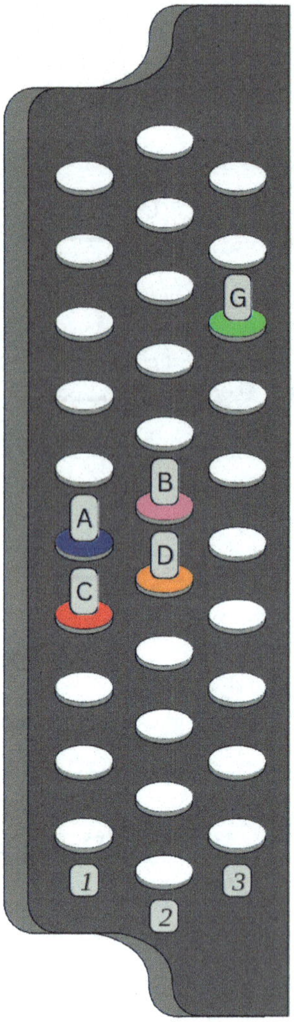

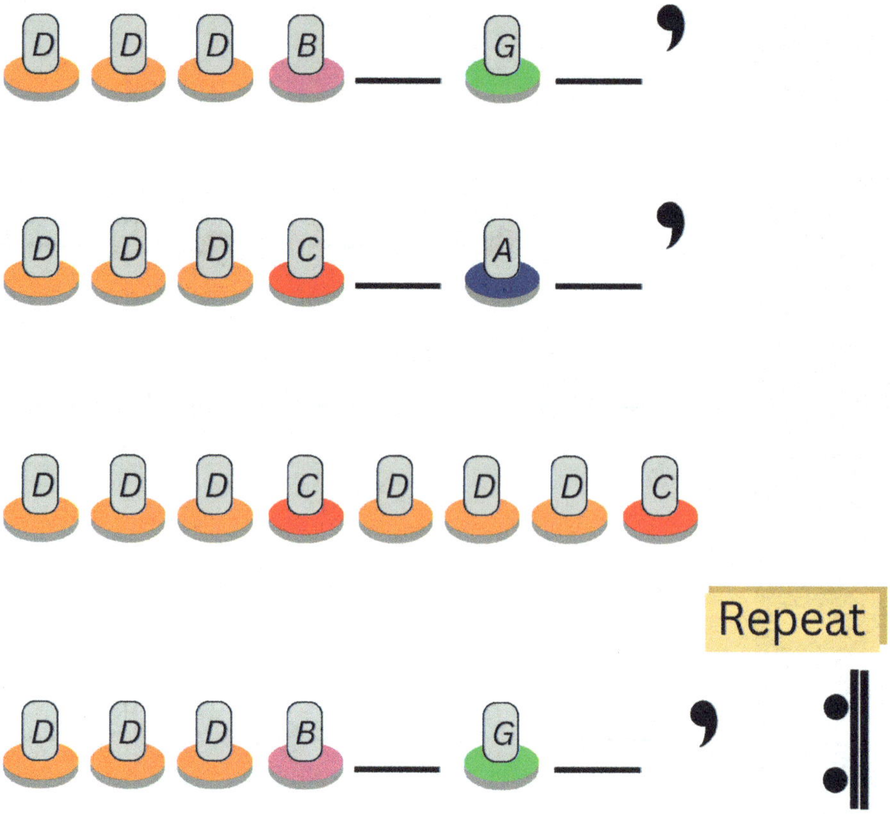

Suggested Fingering

G=Index
A=Middle
B=Middle
C=Ring
D=Ring/
Middle

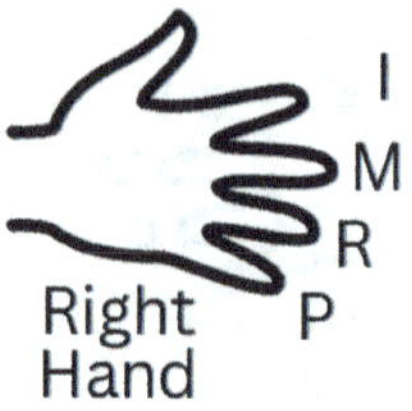

Learning E

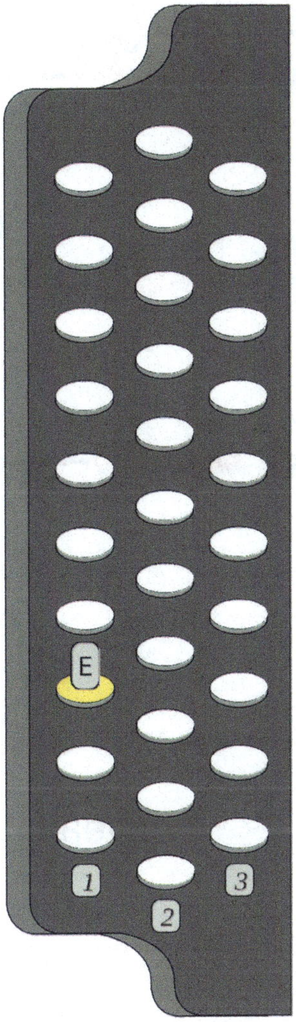

Close bellows

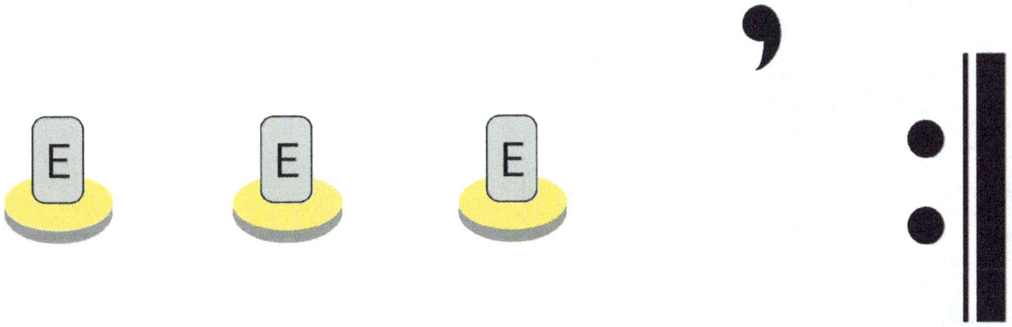

Repeat

Suggested Fingering

E = Middle

Bellows out

Huapango #1

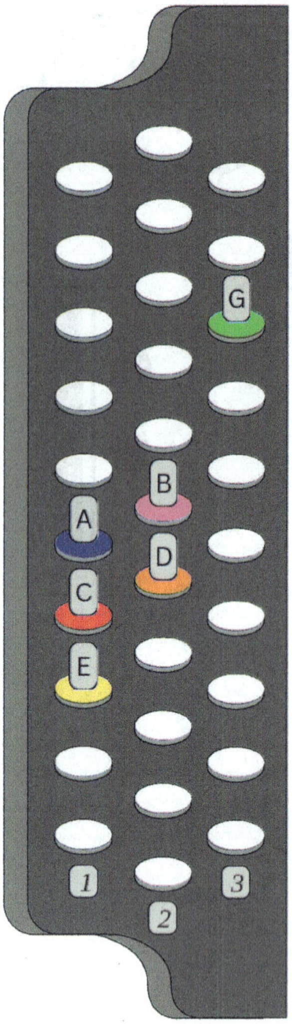

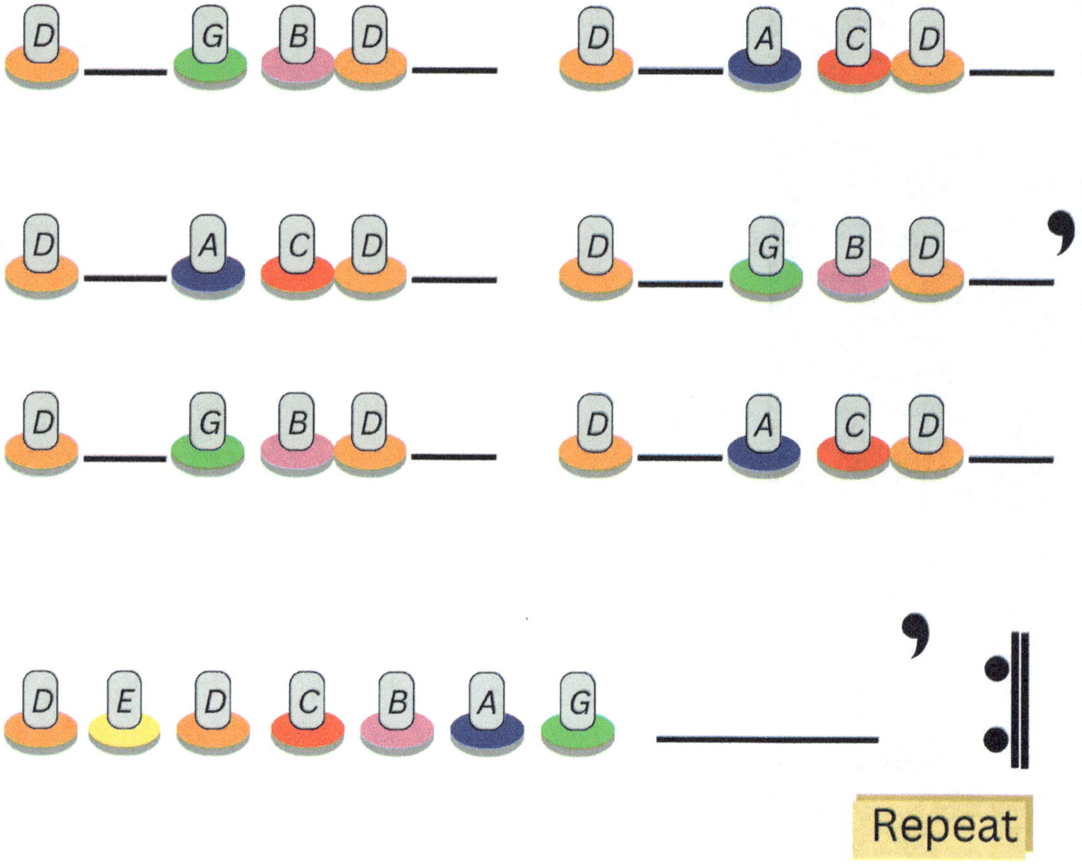

Suggested Fingering

G=Index
A=Ring/Index
B=Middle
C=Ring/Middle
D=Ring/Index
E = Middle

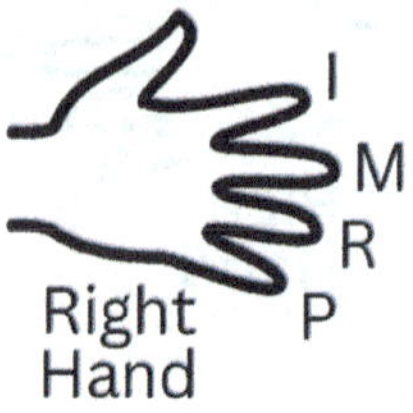

Learning F#

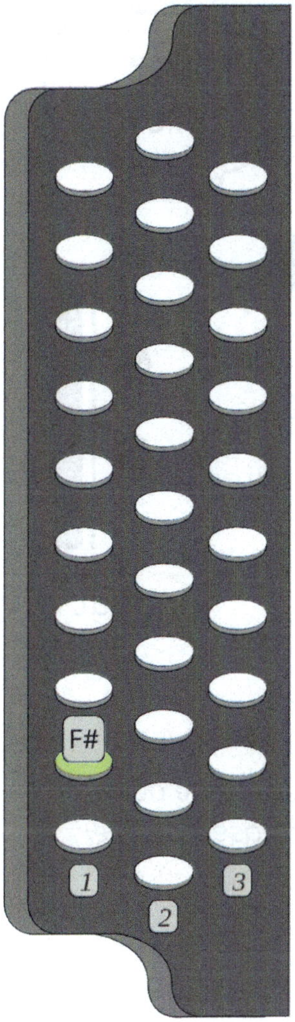

Suggested Fingering

F# = Ring

Learning High "g"

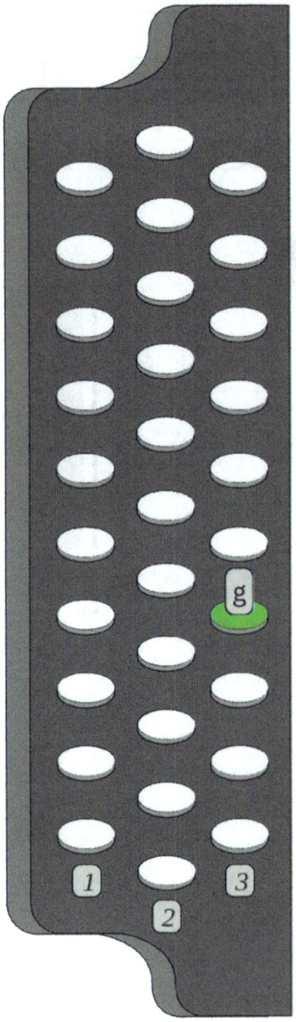

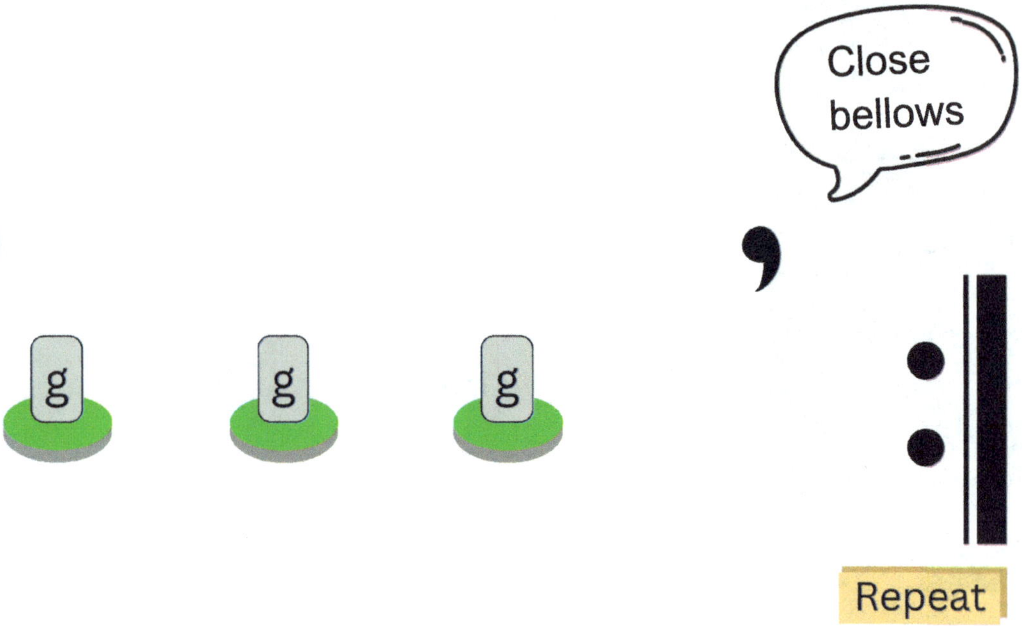

Note: *This is the same pitch class as the other G note, but one octave higher. Since it's an octave G, we'll label it with a lowercase letter (g) to indicate the higher pitch.*

Suggested Fingering

g = Index

I

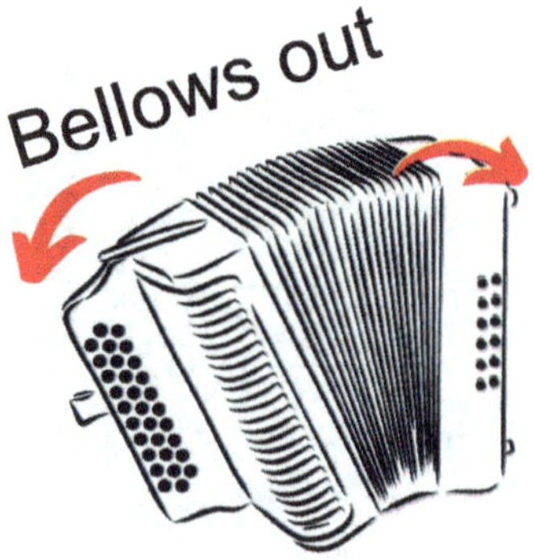

G Major Scale

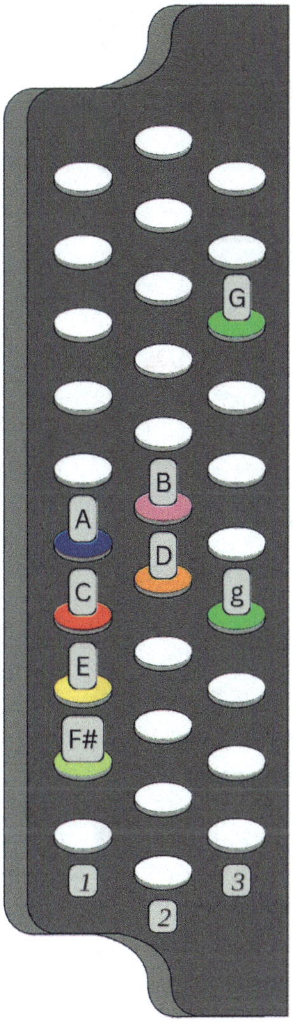

G Ascending

G A B C D E F# g :‖

Repeat

G Descending

g F# E D C B A G :‖

Repeat

G Major Scale

G A B C D E F# g

F# E D C B A G :‖

Repeat

Suggested Fingering

G= Index
A= Ring / Middle
B= Index
C = Middle
D = Index
E = Middle
F# = Ring
g =Index

Adolorido Polka

A Section

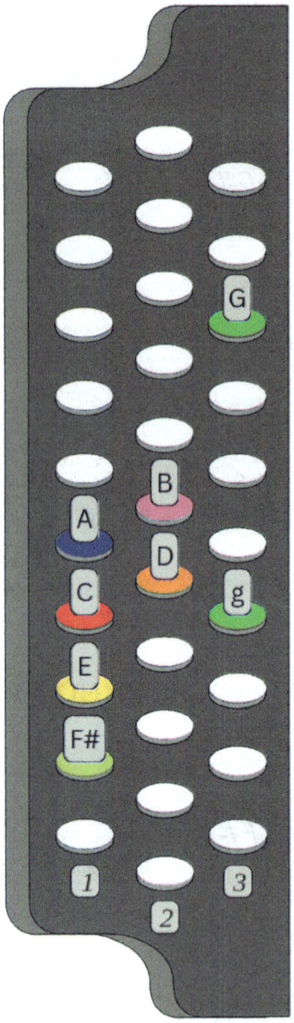

G A B C ___ B ___ ,

G A B C ___ B ___ ,

G A B C ___ B C

D ___ C B A ________ ,

F# F# E E ___ D ___ ,

F# F# E E ___ D ___ ,

F# F# E E ___ D ___ Repeat

C ___ B A G ________ :||

Suggested Fingering

G=Index
A=Ring
B=Middle
C = Ring
D =Middle/Index
E = Miidle
F# = Ring

Adolorido Polka

B Section

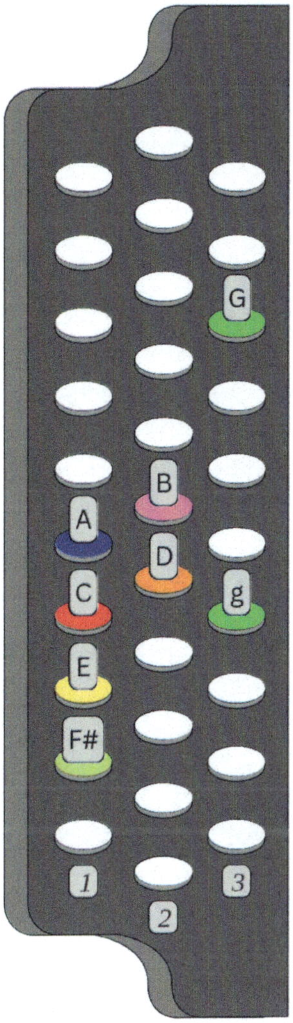

B g F# E D

F# E D C

E D C B A ___ ,

A F# E D C

E D C B

Repeat

D C B A G ___ , :||

Suggested Fingering

G=Index
A=Middle/Ring
B=Index/Middle
C = Middle/Ring
D = Index/Middle
E = Middle
F# = Ring
g =Index

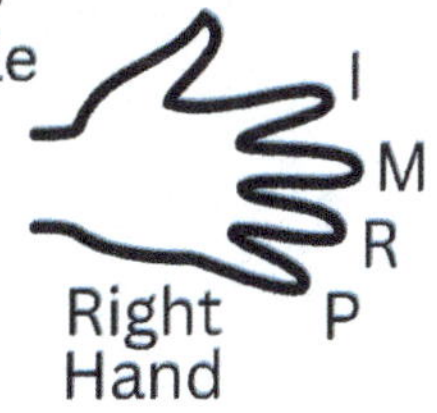

Adolorido Polka

Form

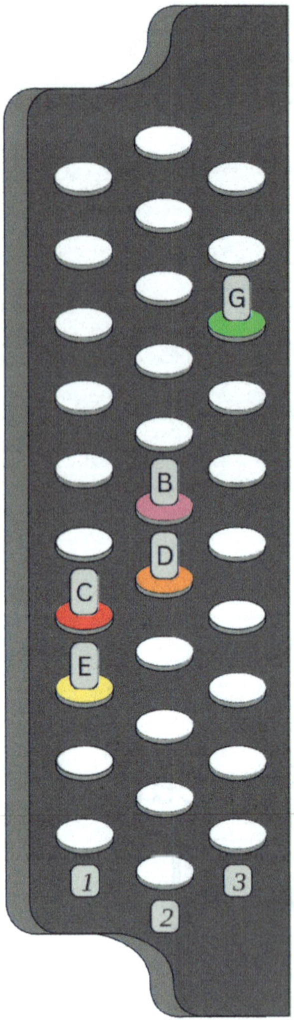

A Section
(with repeat)

B Section
(with repeat)

A Section
(with repeat)

B Section
(with repeat)

A Section
(with repeat)

Ending

Ending

Suggested Fingering

G=Index
B=Middle
C = Ring
D = Middle
E = Ring

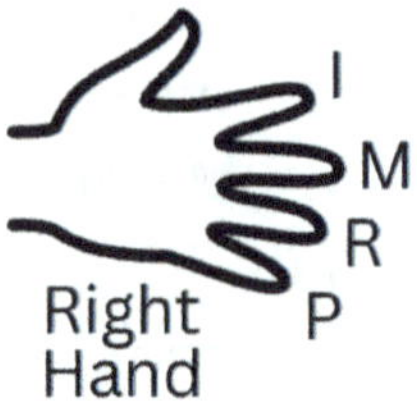

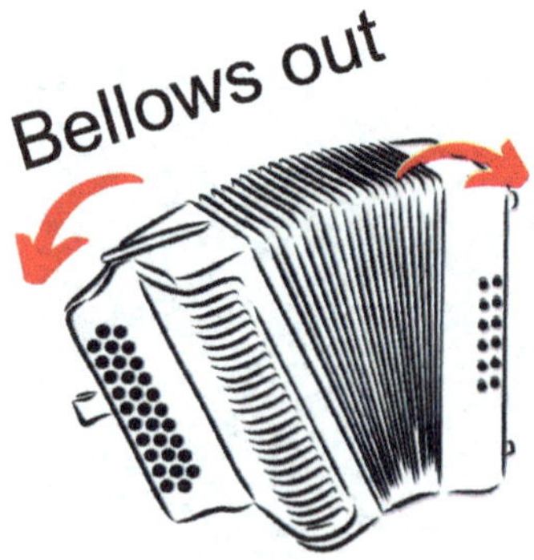

Intentionally left
blank for page turns

Polka 101

A Section

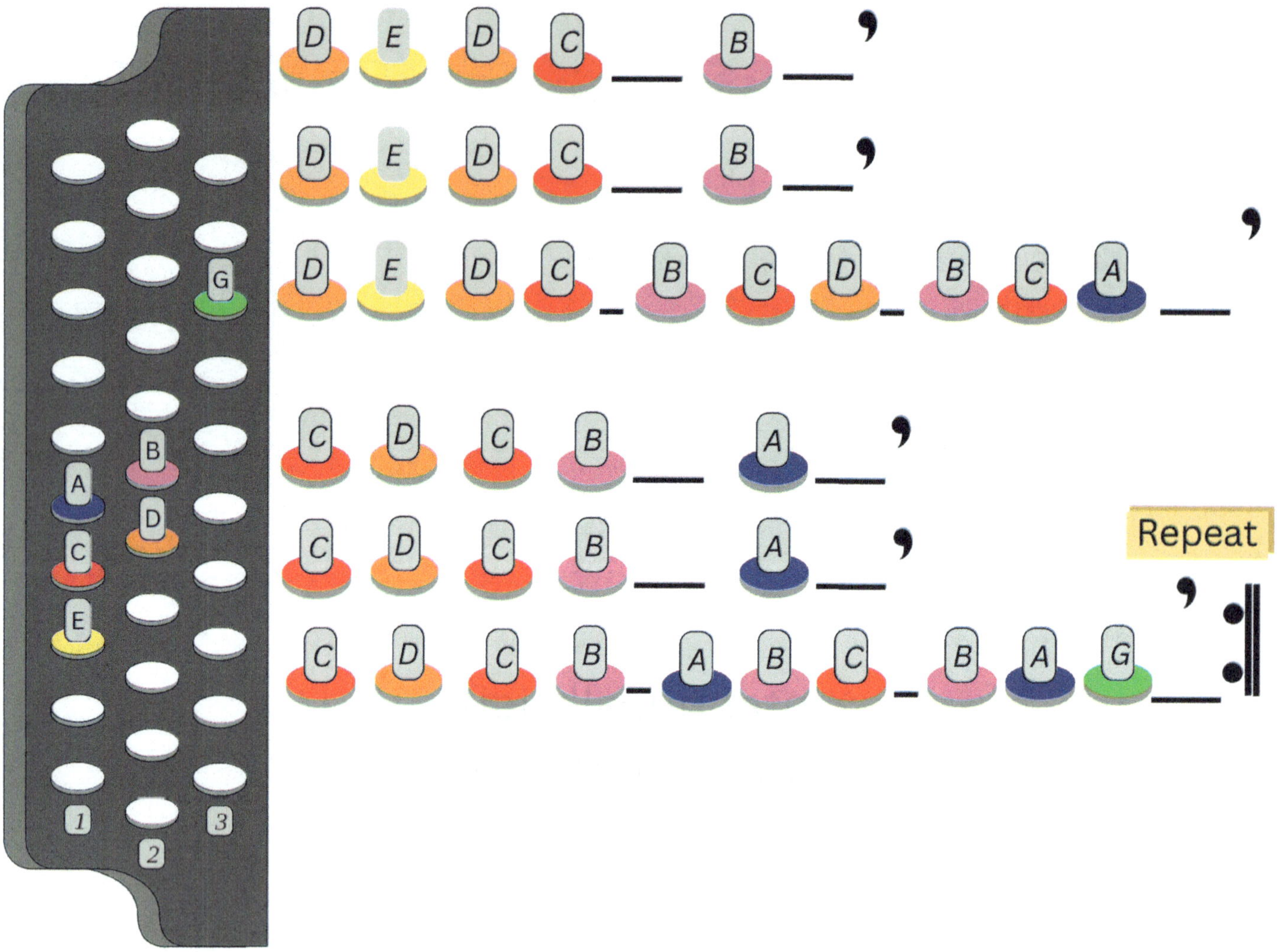

Suggested Fingering

G=Index
A=Middle
B =Index
C = Middle
D = Index
E = Middle

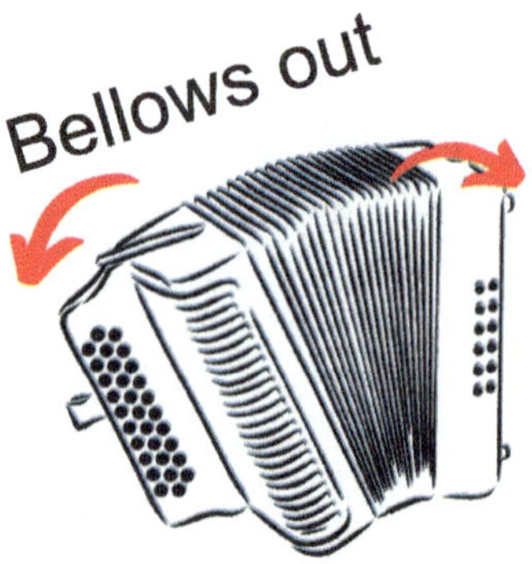

Polka 101

B Section

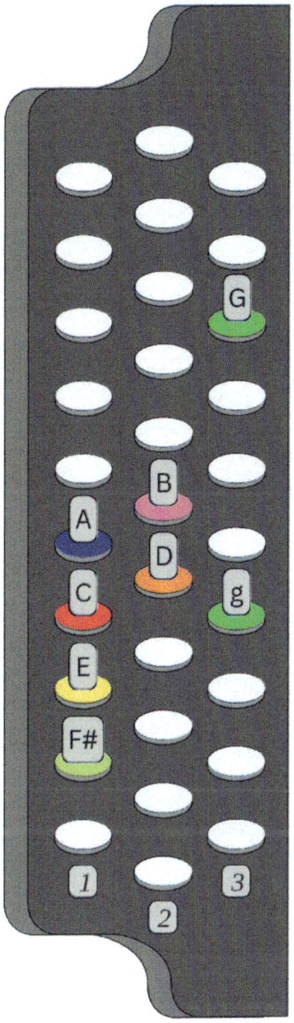

Suggested Fingering

G=Index
A=Middle
B=Index
C = Middle
D = Index
E = Middle
F# = Ring
g = Index

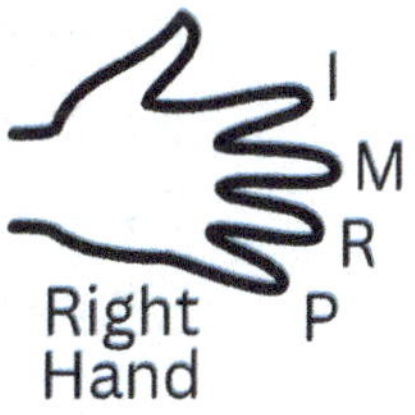

Polka 101

Form

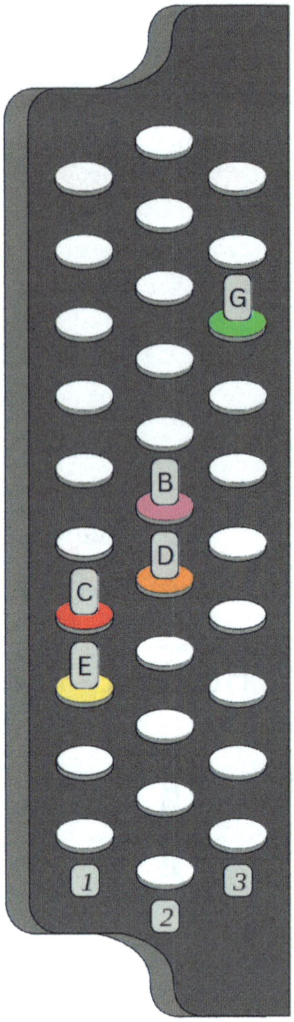

A Section
(with repeat)

B Section
(with repeat)

A Section
(with repeat)

B Section
(with repeat)

A Section
(with repeat)

Ending

Suggested Fingering

G=Index
A=Middle
B=Index
C = Middle
D = Index
E = Middle
F# = Ring
g = Index

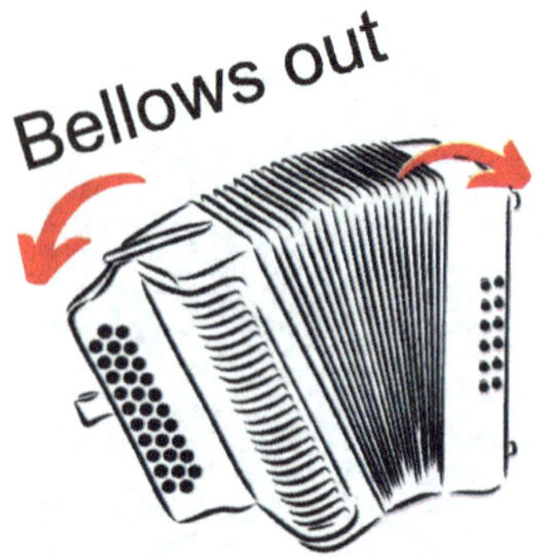

Double Stops

Double stops occur when you play **two notes at the same time,** creating a harmony. Typically, one of the notes is the root note, and the other forms the harmony.
In this example, the root note is **G**, and the harmony note is **B**.

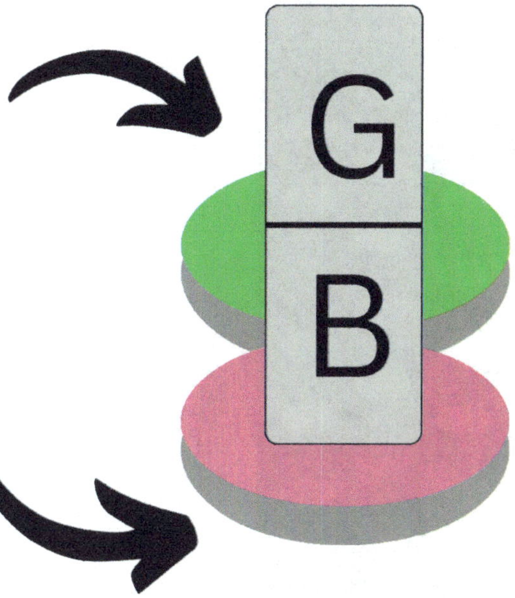

Play both notes at the same time.

Learning G / B

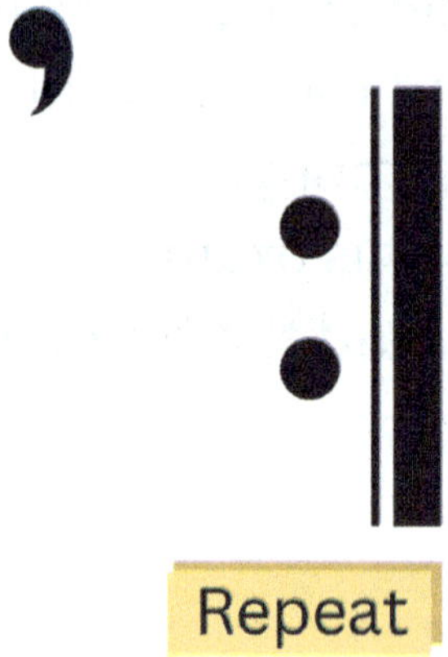

Suggested Fingering

G / B = I / M

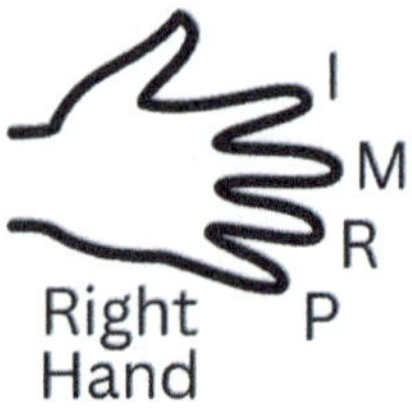

Learning A / C

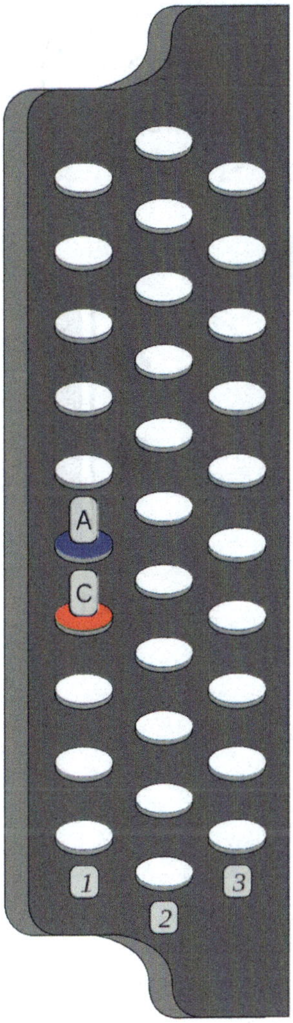

Suggested Fingering

A / C = M / R

Learning B / D

Suggested Fingering

B / D = M / R

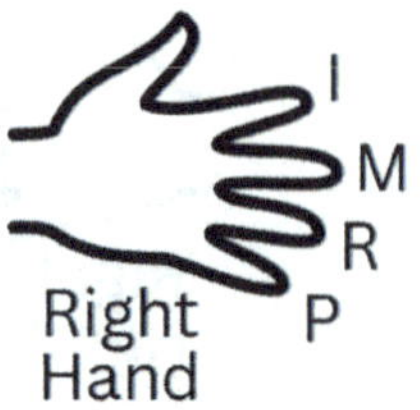

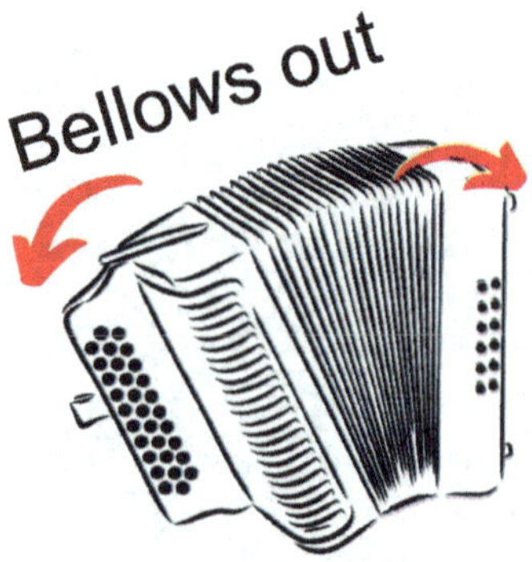

Polka #1

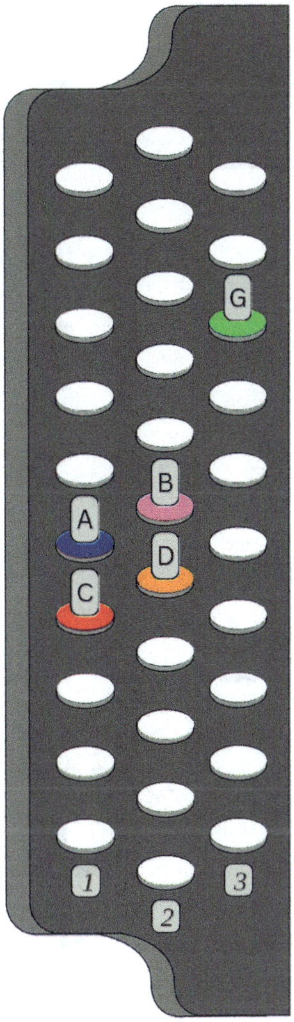

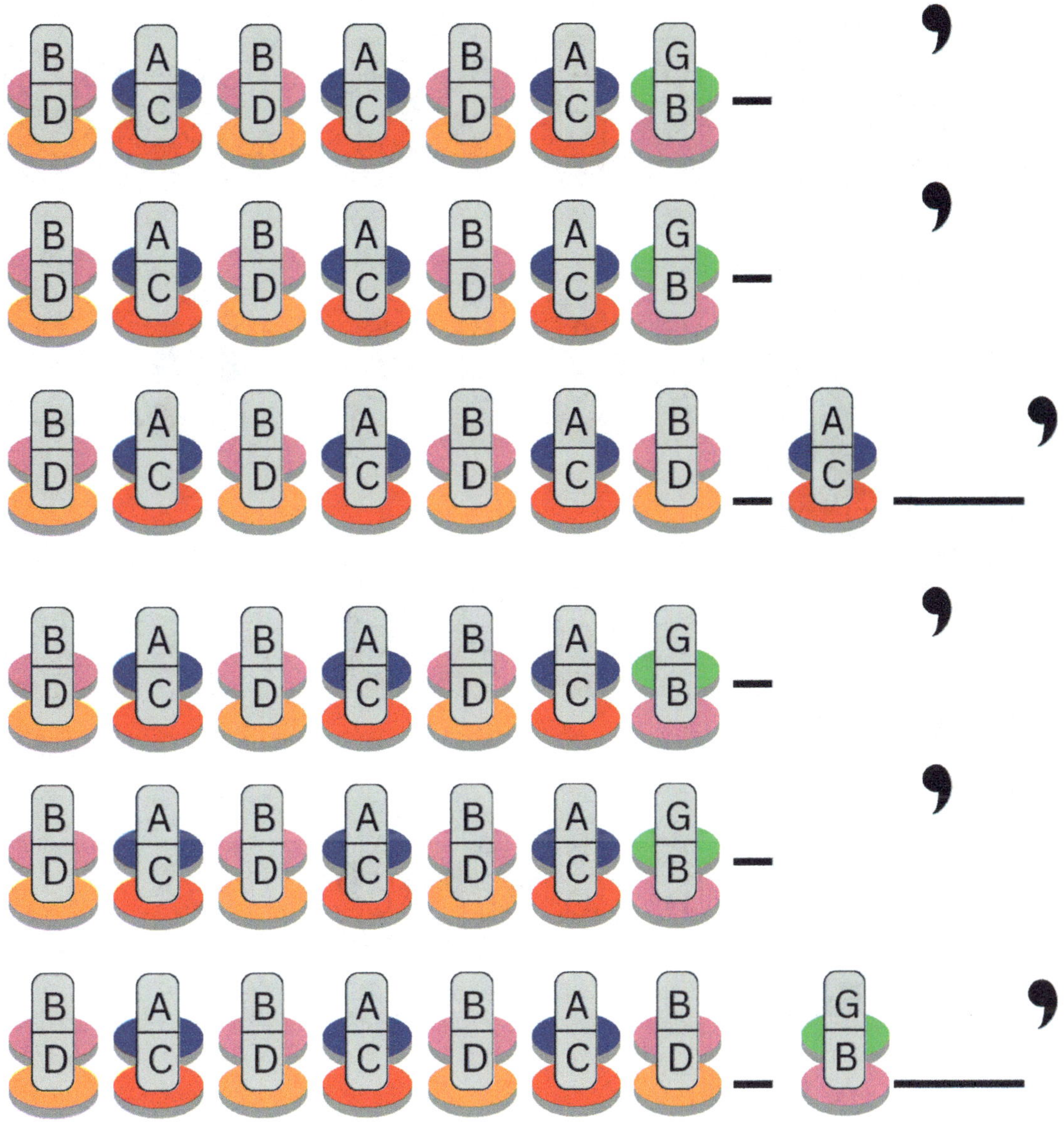

Suggested Fingering

G / B = I / M

A / C = M / R

B / D = M / R

Polka #2

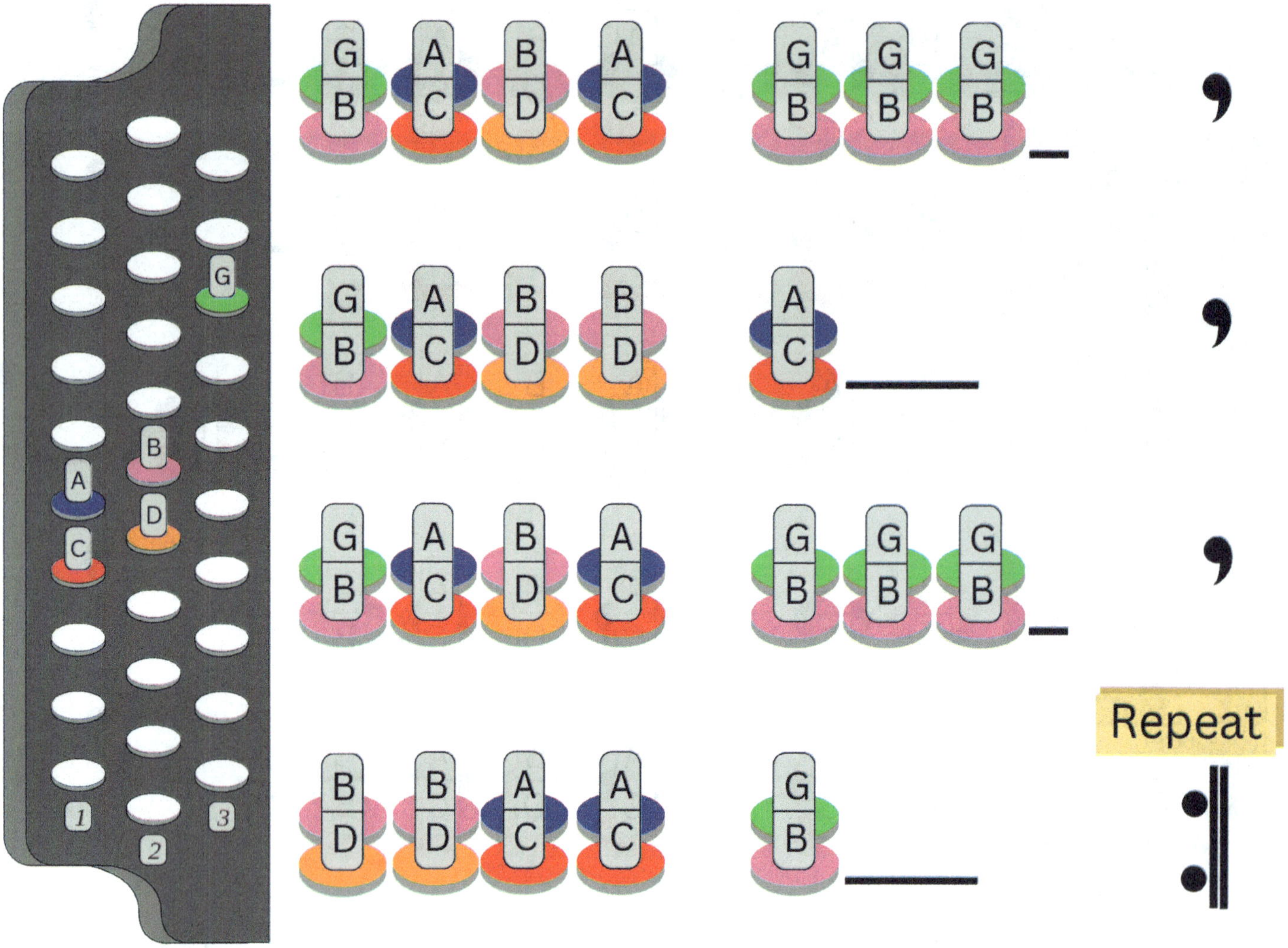

Suggested Fingering

G / B = I / M
A / C = M / R
B / D = M / R

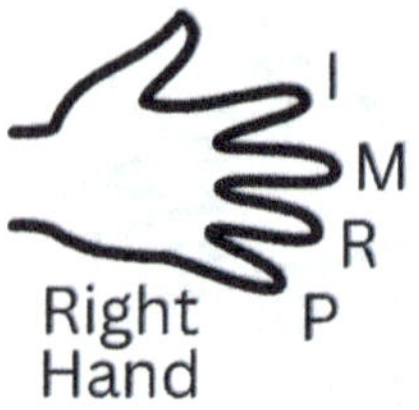

Cumbia #1

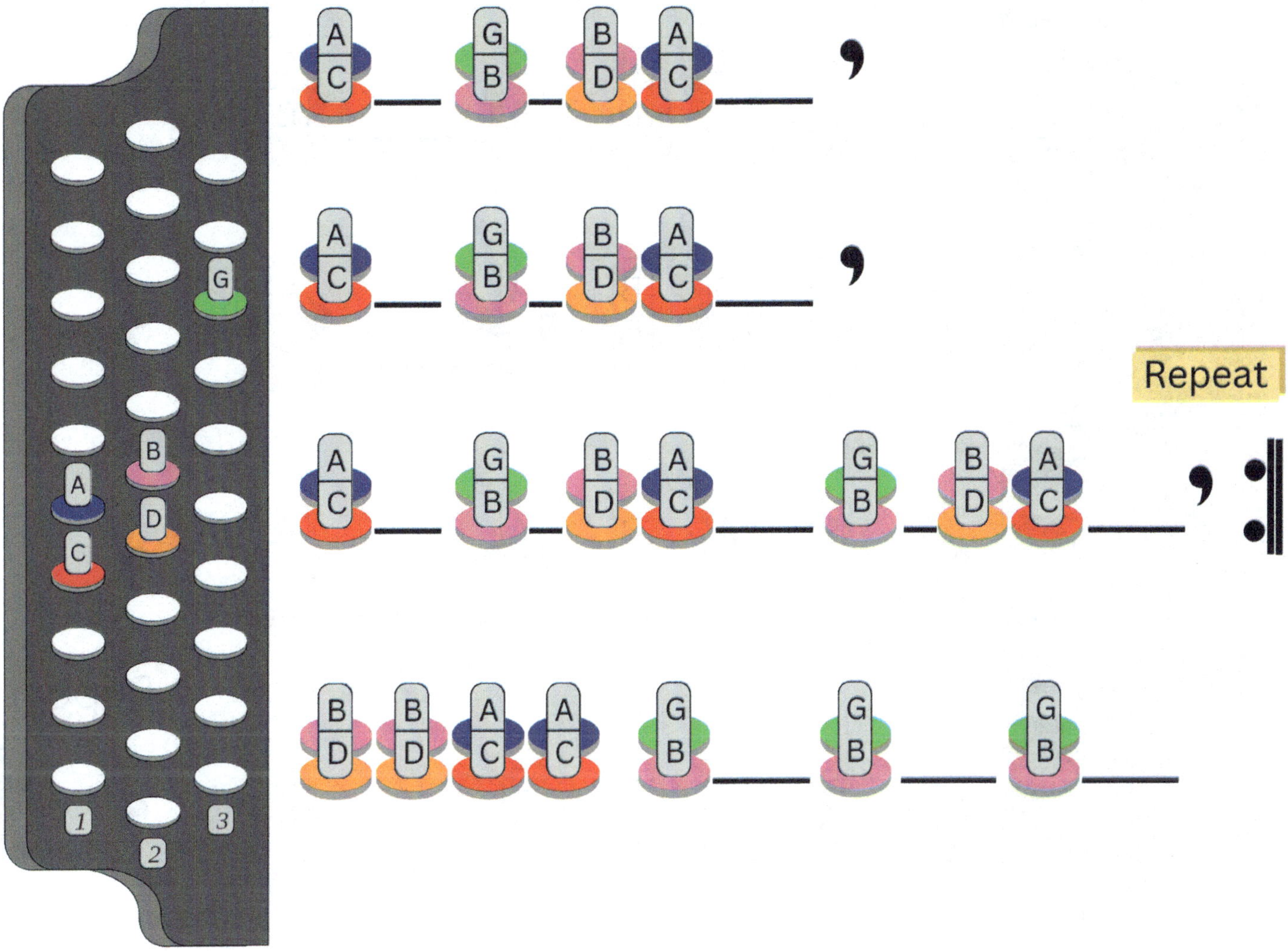

Suggested Fingering

G / B = I / M

A / C = M / R

B / D = M / R

Cumbia #2

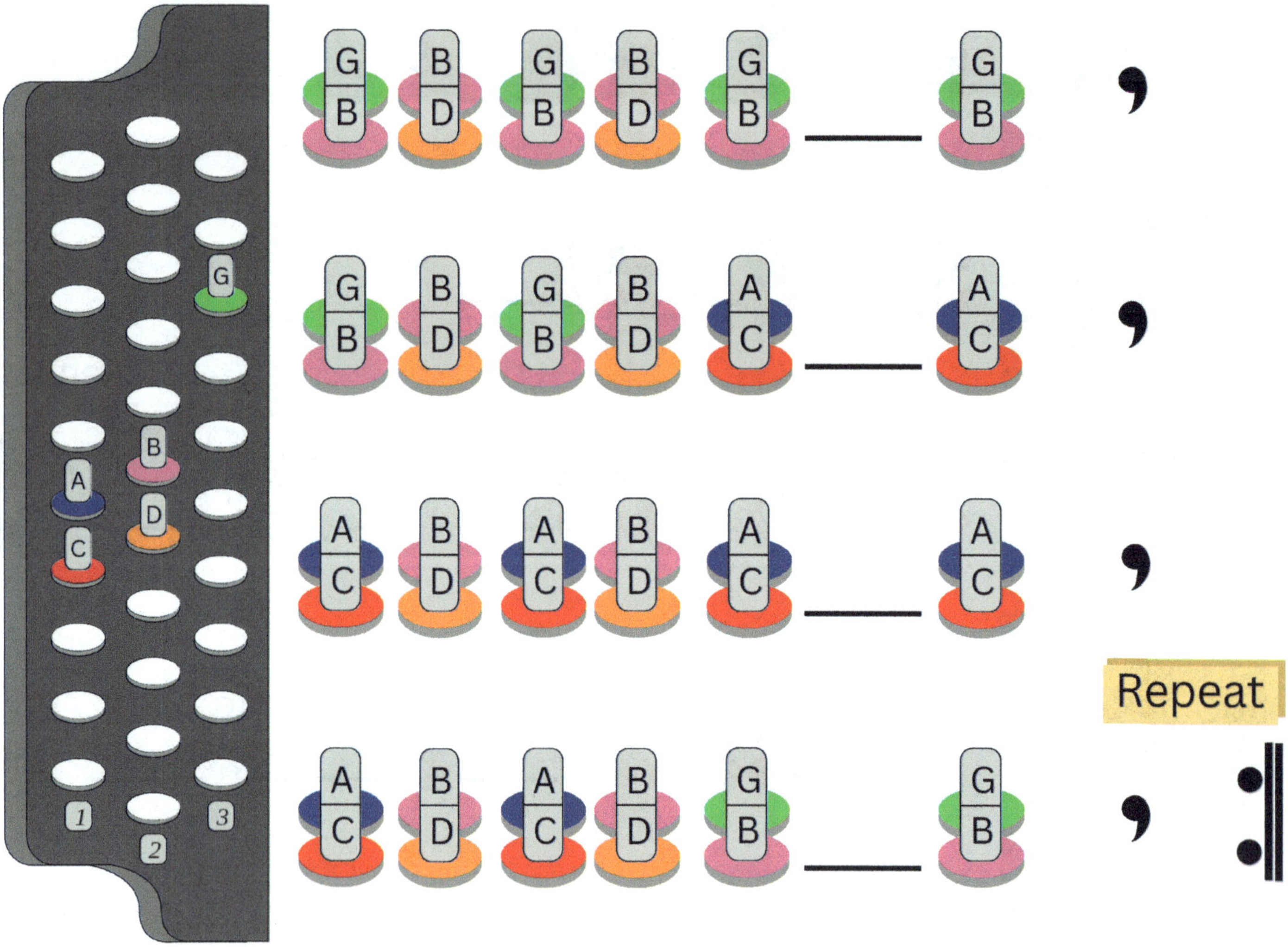

Suggested Fingering

G / B = I / M

A / C = M / R

B / D = M / R

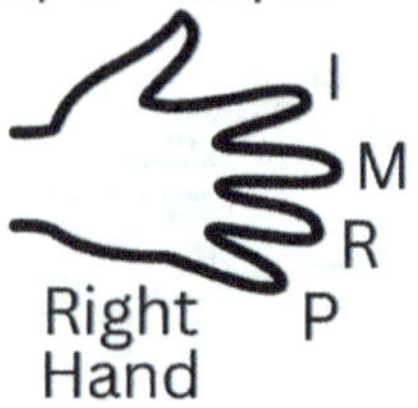

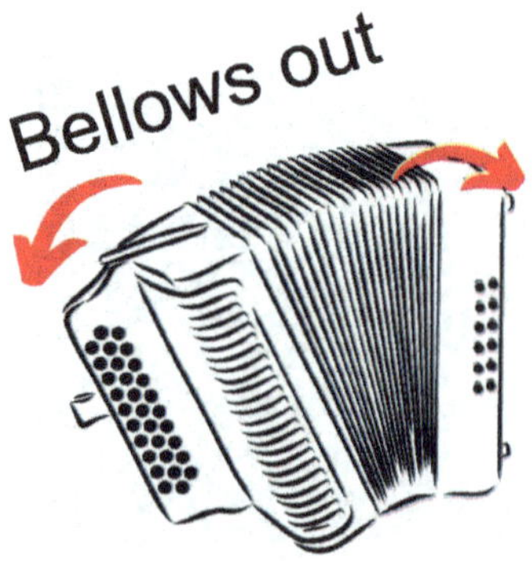

Learning C / E

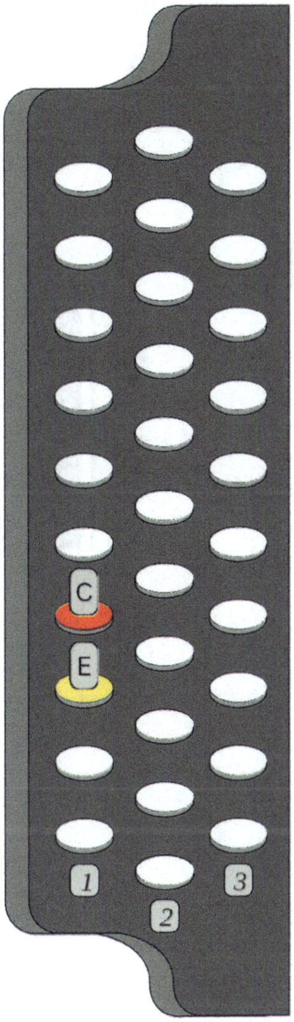

Suggested Fingering

C / E = M / R

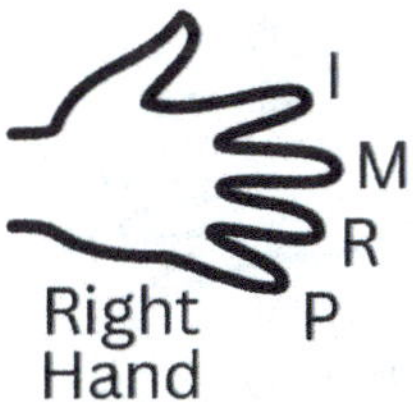

Learning D / F#

Close bellows

Repeat

Suggested Fingering

D / F# = I / R

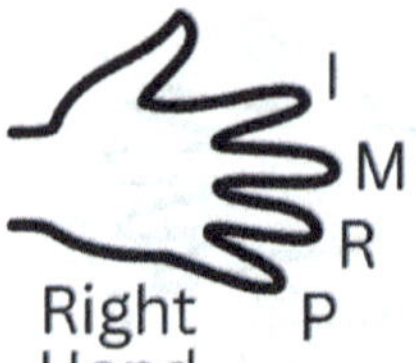

G Major - 5 notes

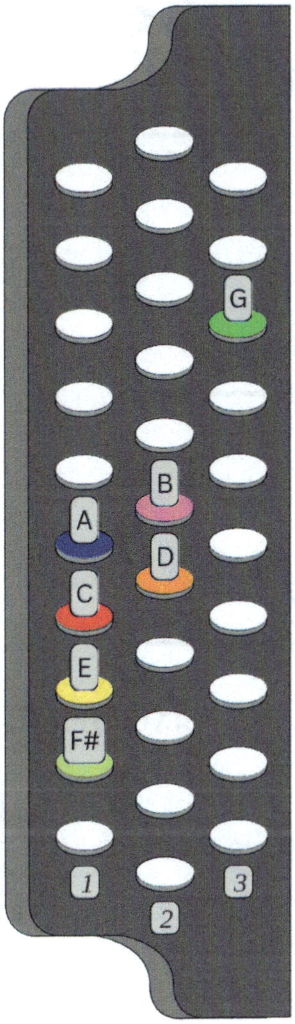

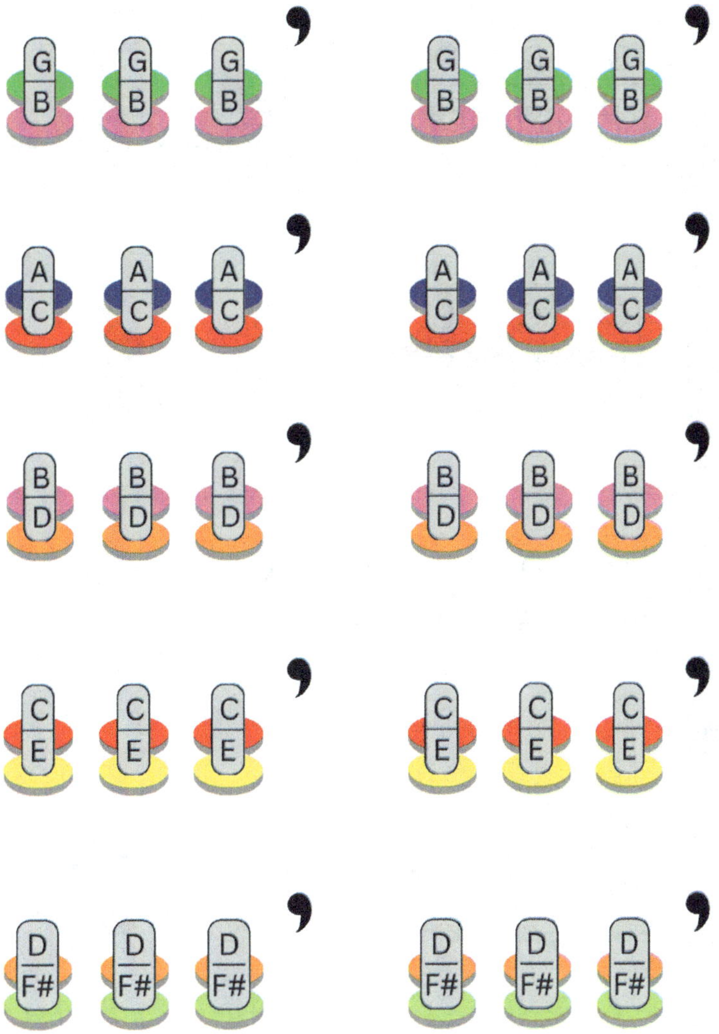

Suggested Fingering

G / B = I / M
A / C = M / R
B / D = I / M
C / E = M / R
D / F# = I / R

Polka #3

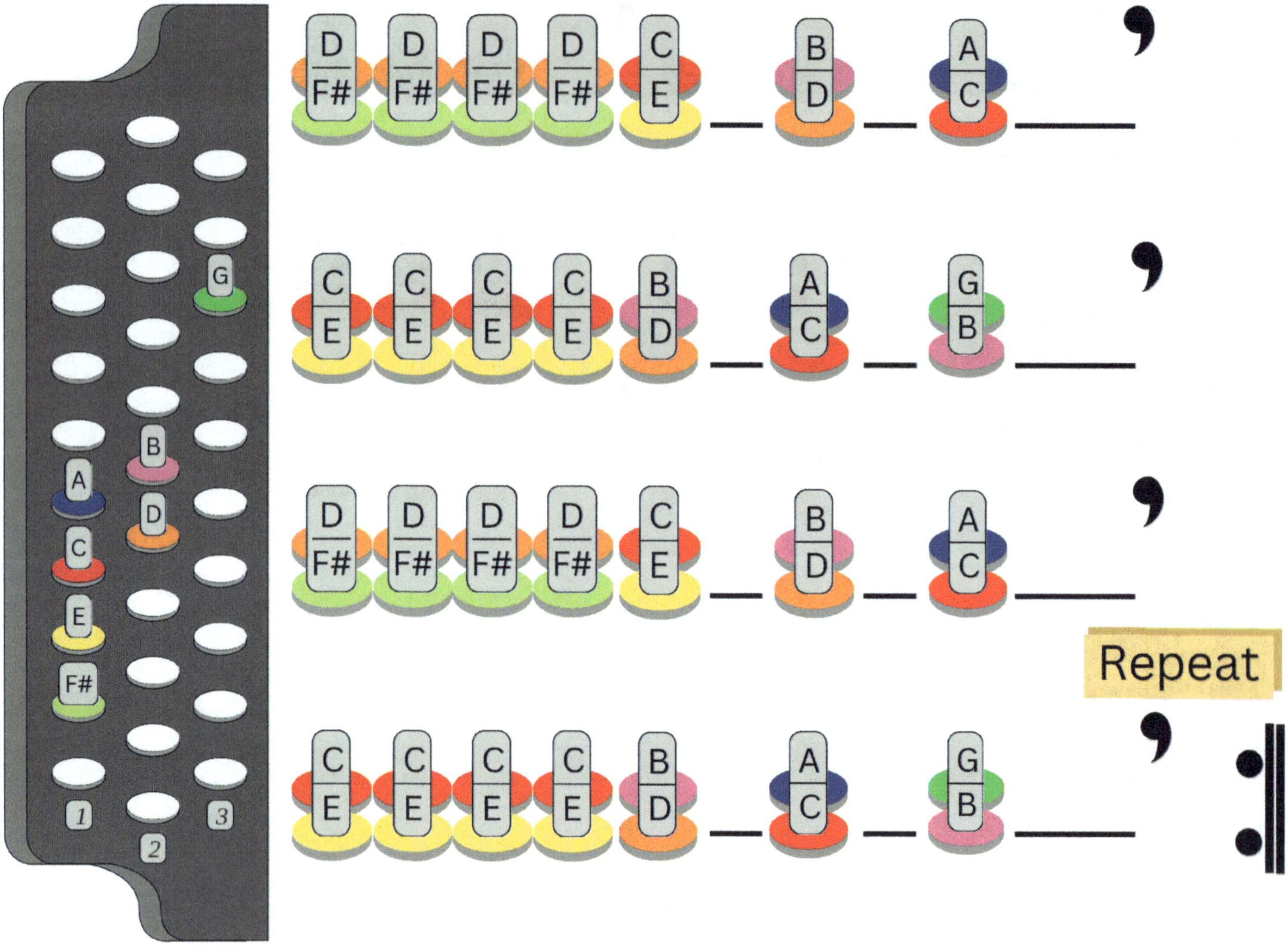

Suggested Fingering

G / B = I / M
A / C = M / R
B / D = I / M
C / E = M / R
D / F# = I / R

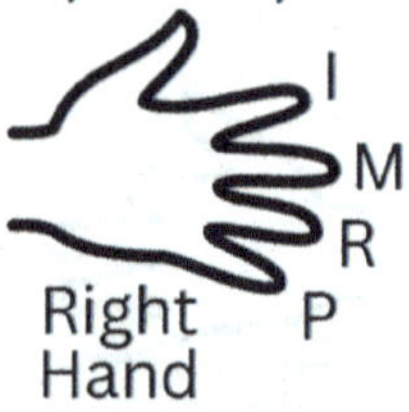

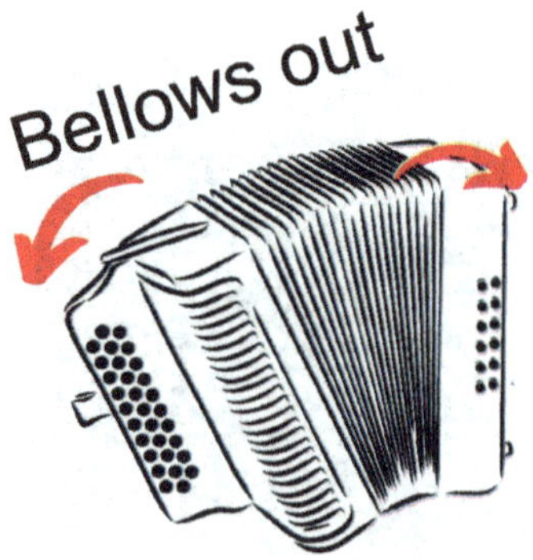

Cumbia #3

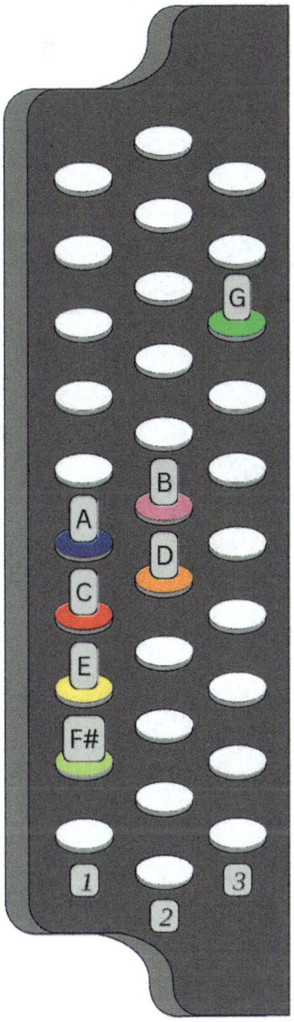

B/D   B/D D/F# B/D

A/C   A/C C/E A/C ,

A/C   A/C C/E A/C

Repeat

G/B   B/D   G/B ___ ,   :||

Ending

G/B ___

Suggested Fingering

G / B = I / M
A / C = I / M
B / D = I / M
C / E = M / R
D / F# = I / R

Polka #4

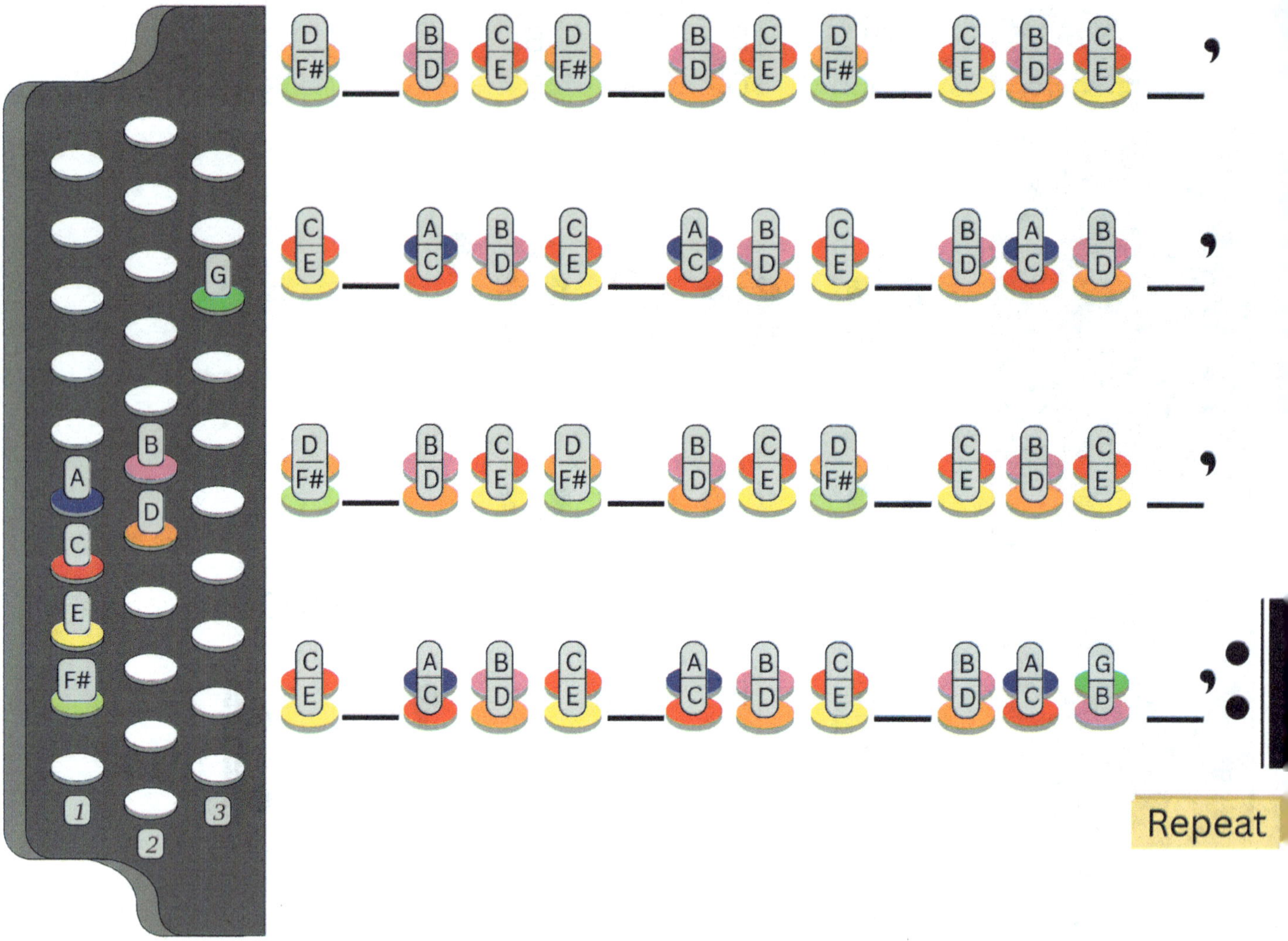

Suggested Fingering

G / B = I / M

A / C = I / M

B / D = I / M

C / E = M / R

D / F# = I / R

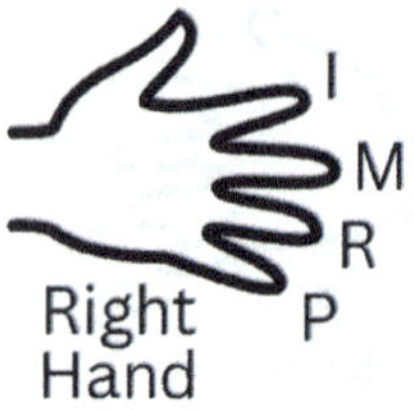

Learning E / g

Note: *This is an alternate E note—it has the same pitch as the other E but is located on a different button in the third row. Using this alternate E can make it easier to play double stops and improve finger positioning in certain passages.*

Suggested Fingering

E / g = I / M

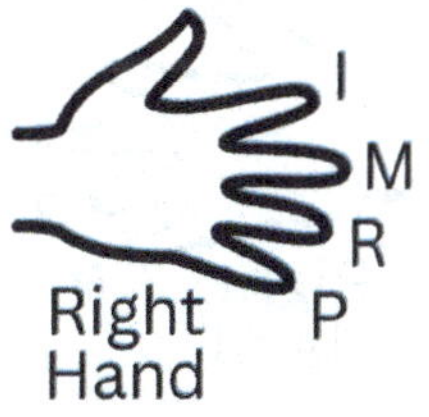

Learning F# / a

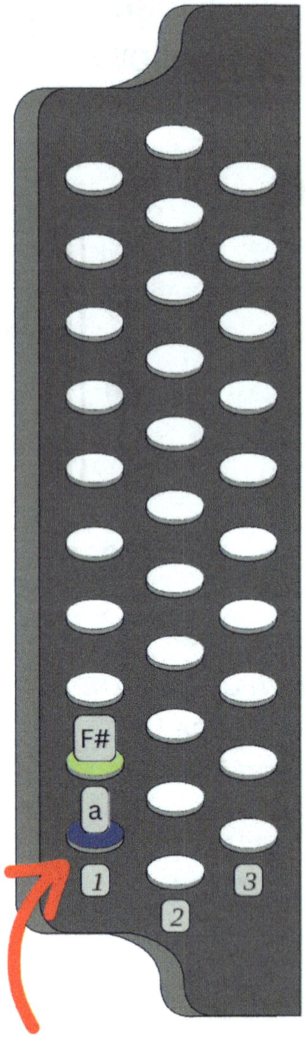

***New note alert!* Octave higher A labeled with a lowercase letter (a).**

Suggested Fingering

F# / a = M / R

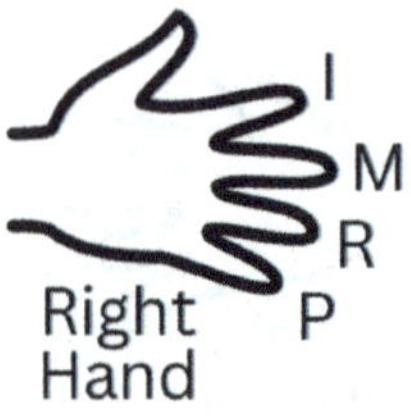

Learning g / b

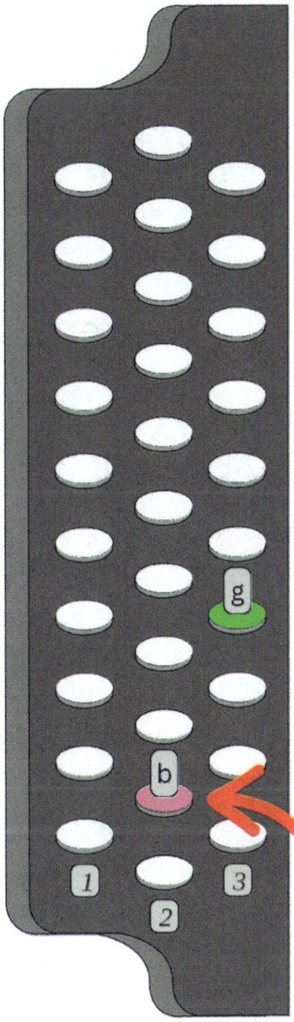

Repeat

New note alert! ***Octave higher B labeled with a lowercase letter (b).***

Suggested Fingering

g / b = I / M

G Major

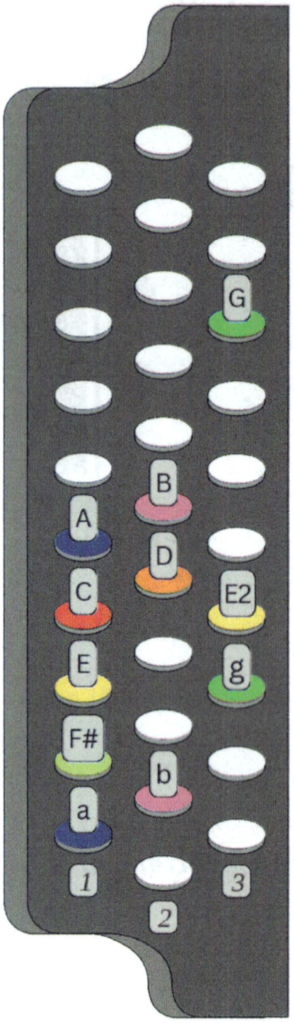

G Ascending

Repeat

G Descending

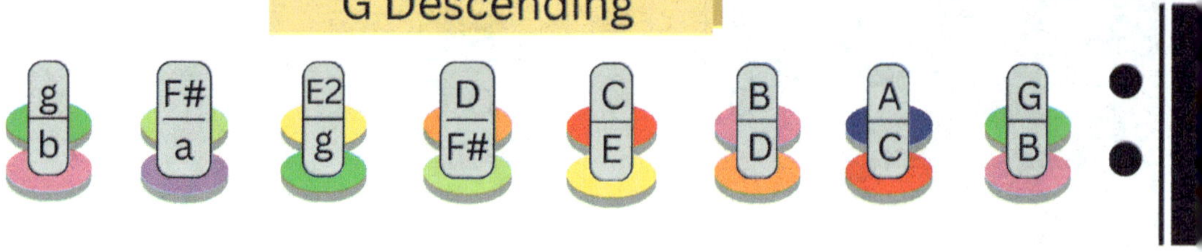

Repeat

G Major Scale

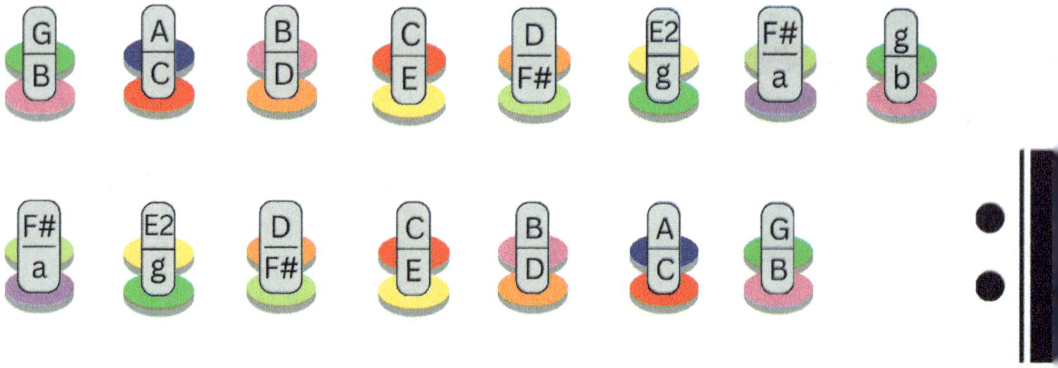

Repeat

Suggested Fingering

G / B = I / M
A / C = M / R
B / D = I / M
C / E = M / R
D / F# = I / R
E2 / g = I / M
F# / a = M / R
g / b = I / M

Intentionally left
blank for page turns

Adolorido Polka

Section A

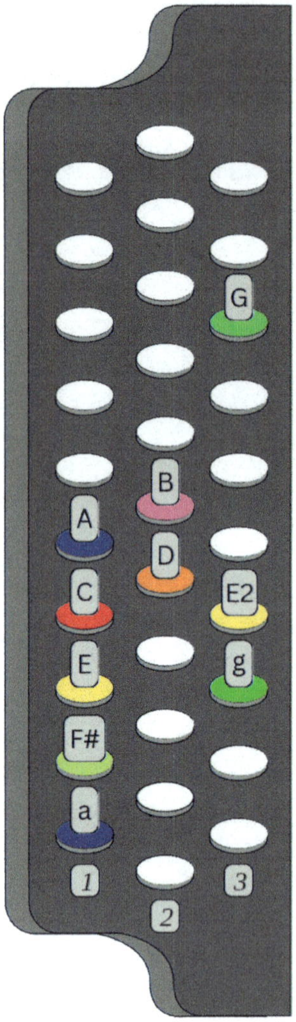

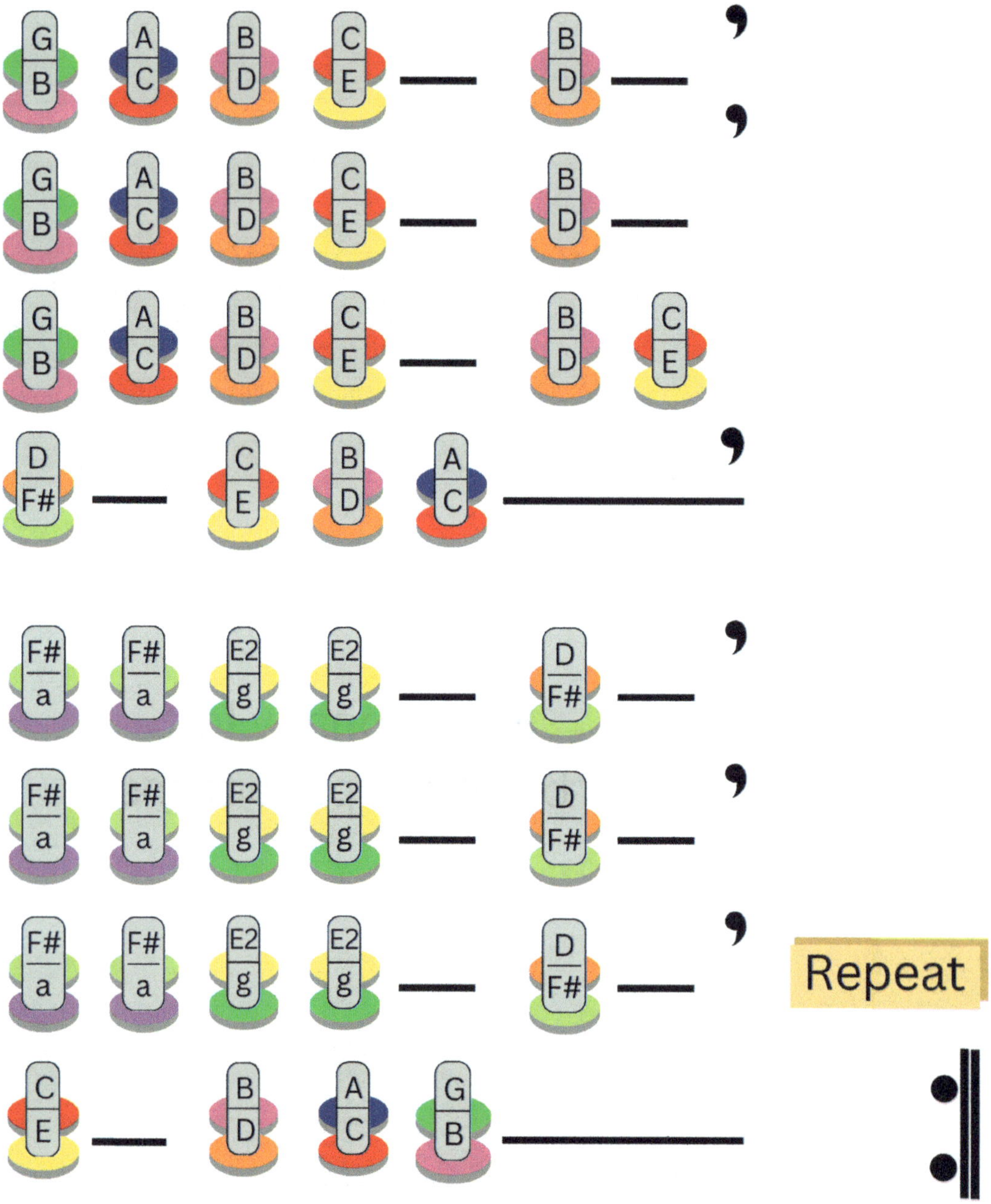

Suggested Fingering

G / B = I / M
A / C = M / R
B / D = I / M
C / E = M / R
D / F# = I / R
E / g = I / M
F# / a = M / R
g / b = I / M

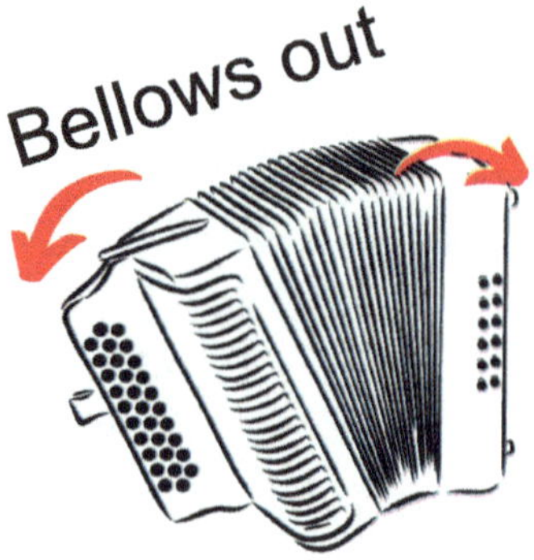

Adolorido Polka

Section B

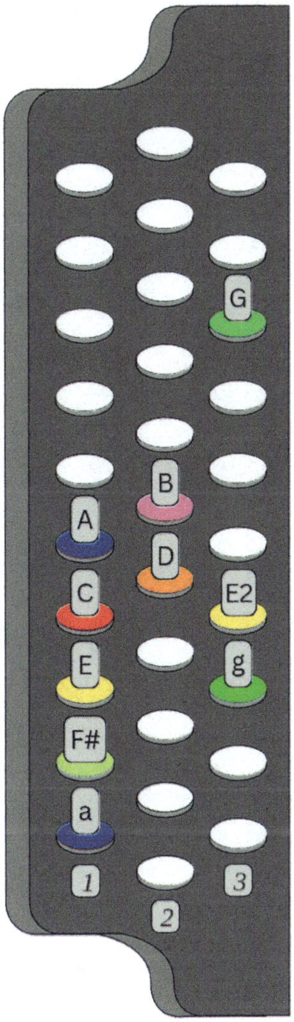

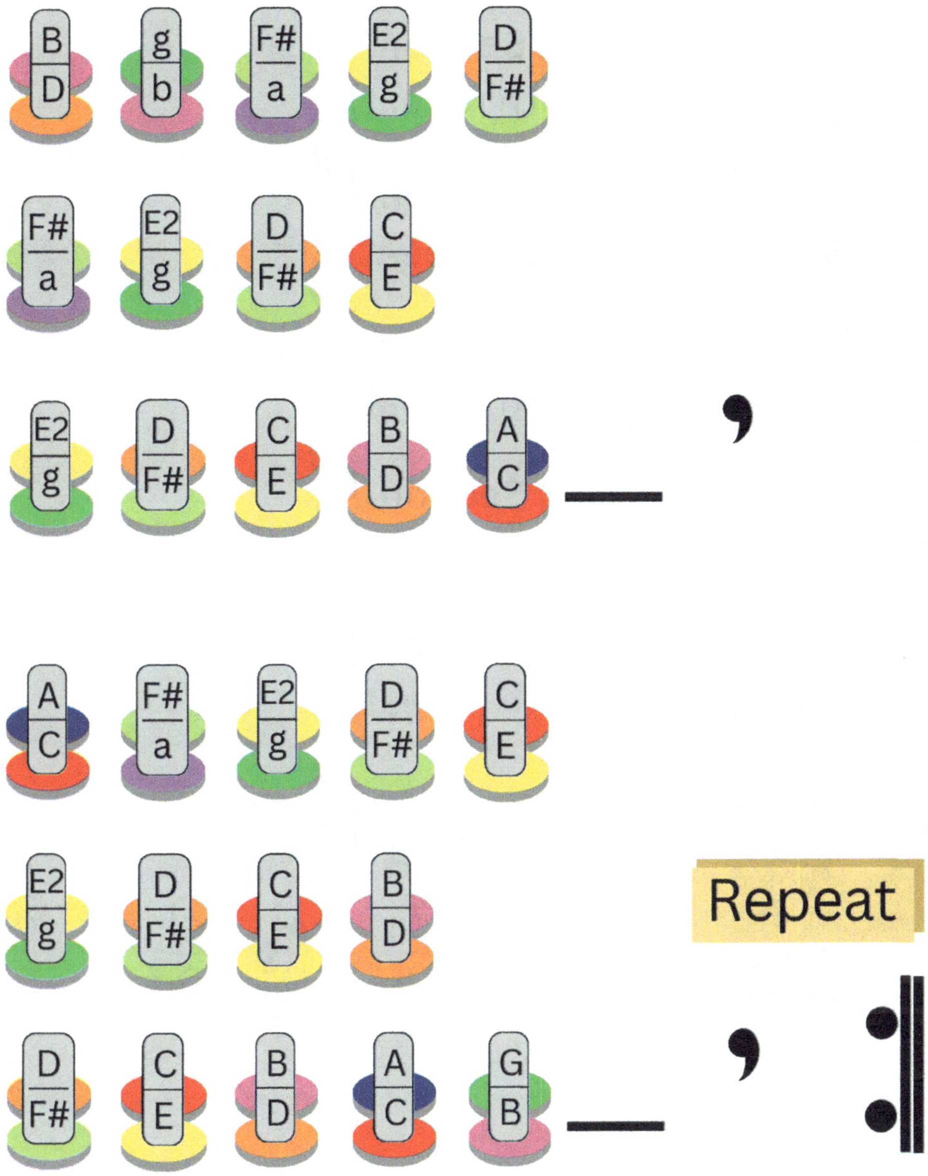

Repeat

Suggested Fingering

G / B = I / M
A / C = M / R
B / D = I / M
C / E = M / R
D / F# = I / R
E / g = I / M
F# / a = M / R
g / b = I / M

Adolorido Polka

Form

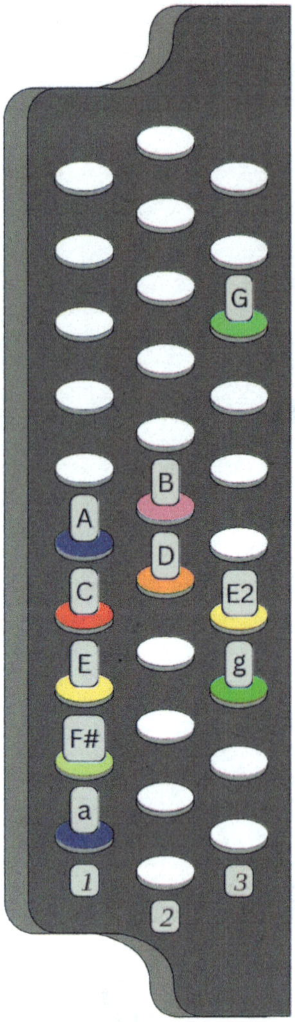

A Section
(with repeat)

B Section
(with repeat)

A Section
(with repeat)

B Section
(with repeat)

A Section
(with repeat)

Ending

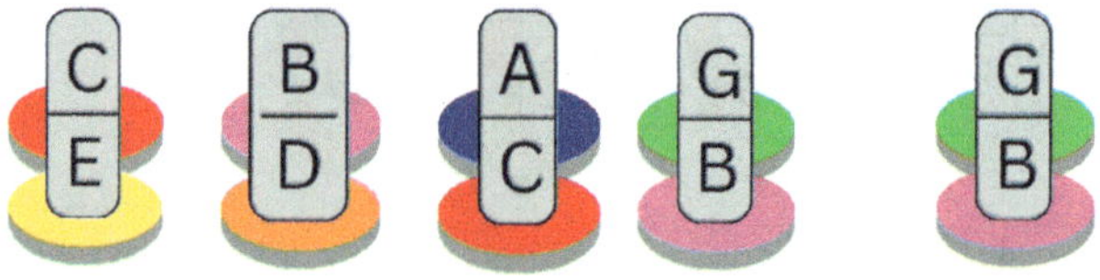

Suggested Fingering

G / B = I / M
A / C = M / R
B / D = I / M
C / E = M / R

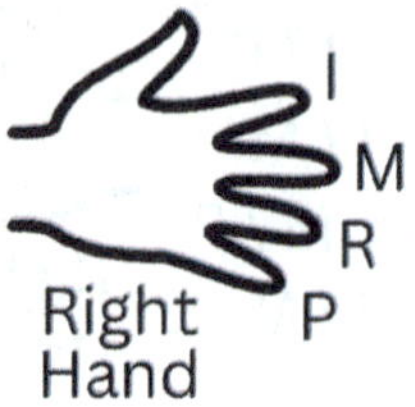

G Major Chord

These chords are built of 3 notes at the same time. Practice hitting the 3 buttons at the same time to create a chord. Notes **G, B,** and **D.**

This is a **G Major Chord.**

Suggested Fingering

G = Index
B = Middle
D = Ring

D Major Chord

These chords are built of 3 notes at the same time. Practice hitting the 3 buttons at the same time to create a chord. Notes **D, F#,** and **A.**

This is a **D Major Chord.**

Suggested Fingering

D = Index
F# = Middle
A = Ring

E Minor Chord

These chords are built of 3 notes at the same time. Practice hitting the 3 buttons at the same time to create a chord. Notes **E, G,** and **B.**

This is a **E Minor Chord.**

Suggested Fingering

E = Index
G = Middle
B = Ring

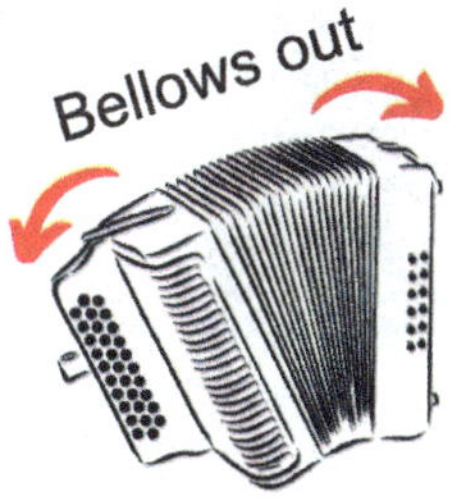

C Major Chord

These chords are built of 3 notes at the same time. Practice hitting the 3 buttons at the same time to create a chord. Notes **C**, **E**, and **G**.

This is a **C Major Chord**.

This chord is played with the **bellows pushed in**. First, open the bellows using the air valve to allow air into the accordion, then press inward to play the notes.

Suggested Fingering

C = Index
E = Middle
G = Ring

Note: BELLOWS IN

Accordion Chords

G Major

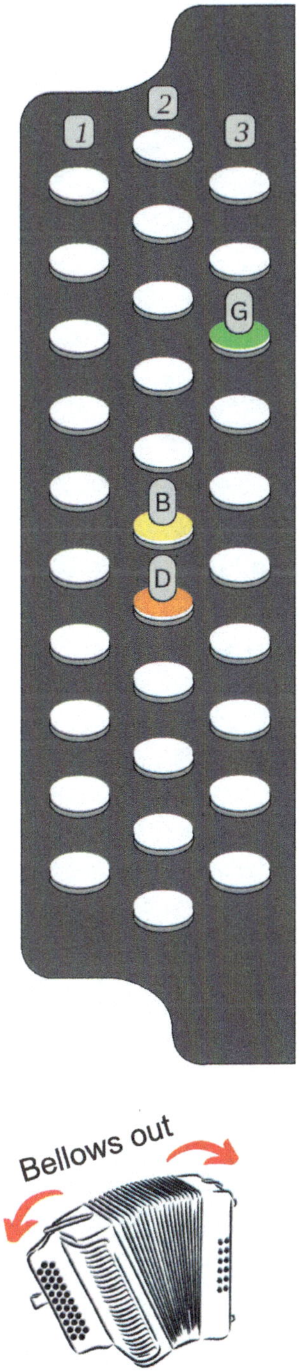

D Major

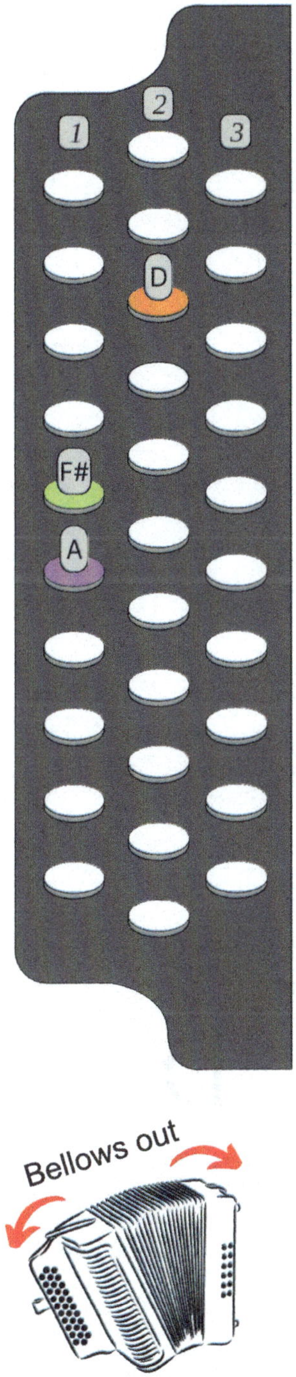

E Minor

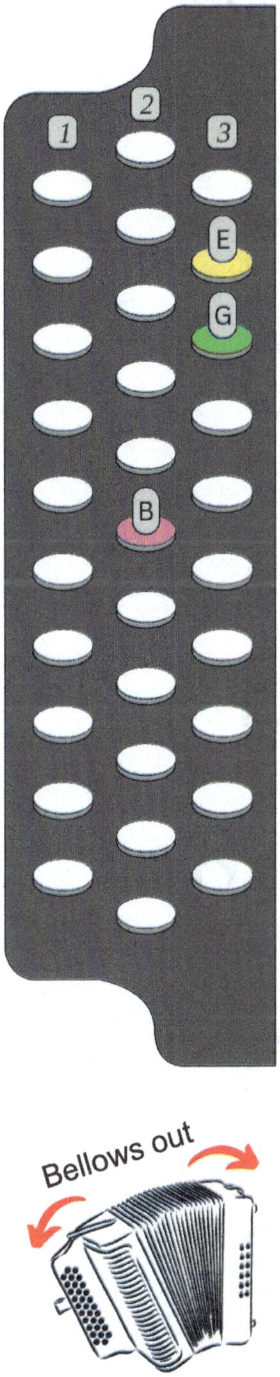

C Major

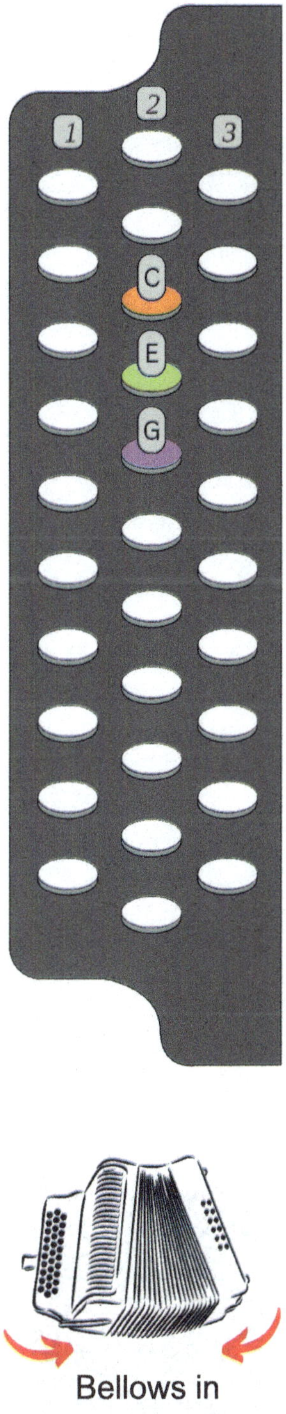

Polka #1 Chords

G

em

C

D

G

em

C D

G

Polka #2 Chords

G				,
G		D		,
G				,
D		G		, Repeat

Cumbia #2 Chords

G				,
G		D		,
D				,
D		G		, Repeat

Accordion Chords

G Major

D Major

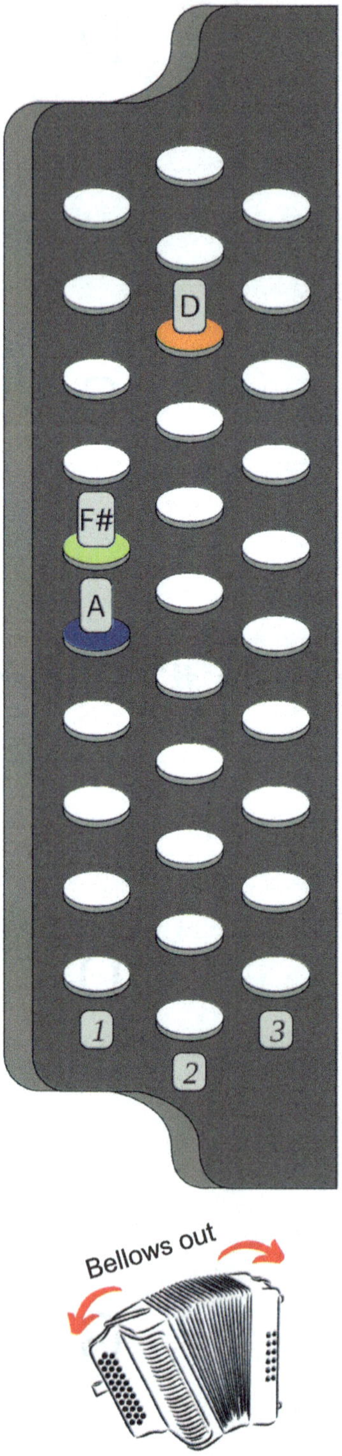

E Minor

Accordion Chords

C Major

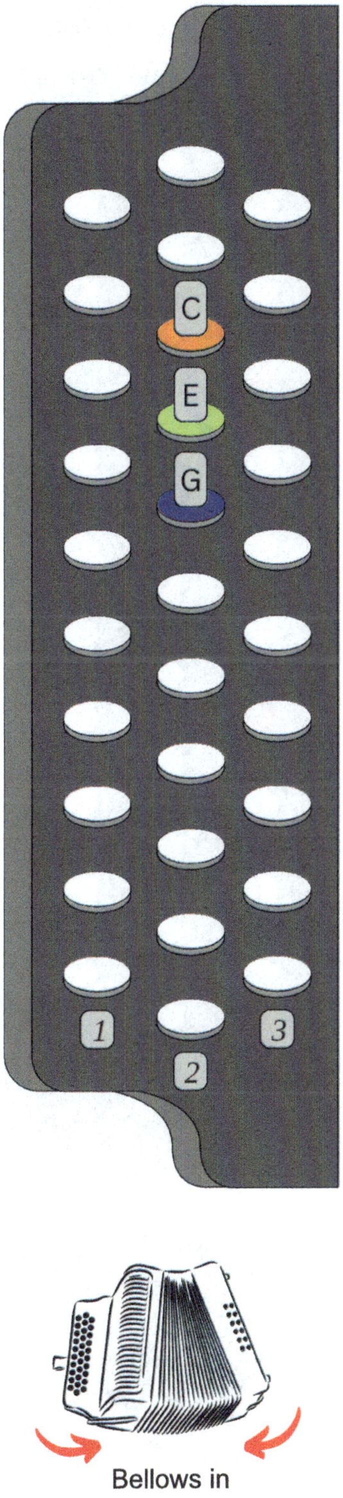

A Minor

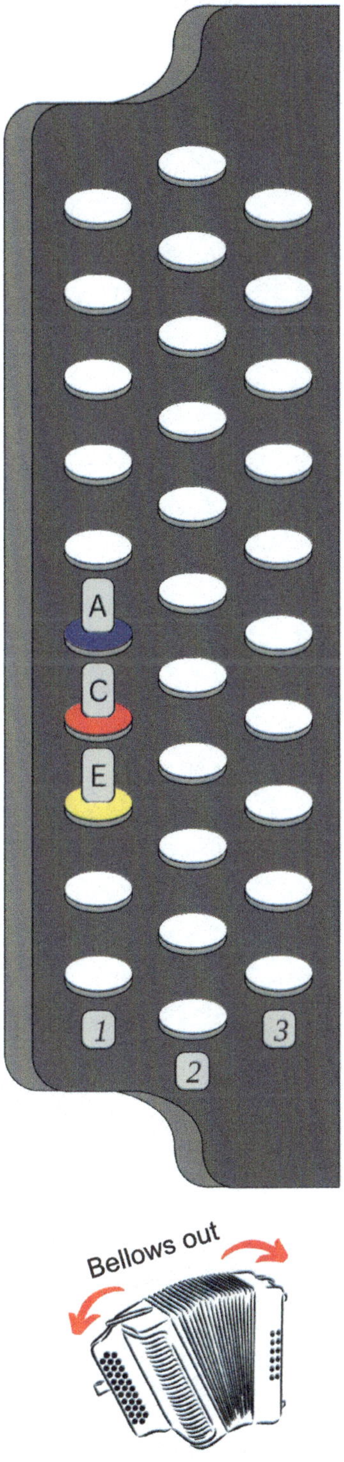

B Minor

Accordion Scales

G Major Scale

G A B C D E F# g

C Major Scale

C D E F G A B c

Accordion Scales

F Major Scale

F G A Bb C D E f

D Major Scale

D E F# G A B C# d

About the Authors
Santiago Castillo

Santiago Castillo, a dedicated music educator with over 18 years of experience, holds a Bachelor's in Music Education from the University of Texas at Brownsville and is currently pursuing his Master's at the University of Texas at Rio Grande Valley. Coming from a family of musicians, he began playing Conjunto music at an early age and developed a deep passion for preserving his cultural heritage.

For over 15 years, Mr. Castillo has been a driving force behind conjunto education, planting the seeds of musical tradition in young elementary school students and ensuring that conjunto music remains alive for future generations. His ability to teach such young musicians with incredible success has earned him widespread respect in the conjunto community. Through his dedication, he has created a legacy, shaped the lives of countless students and inspired them to continue this beautiful musical tradition.

Santiago Castillo

About the Authors cont. Santiago Castillo

Over the past 15 years, his Conjunto programs have earned widespread recognition, including an invitation to perform at TMEA in San Antonio, Texas, in 2017. Santiago currently teaches elementary music in Los Fresnos CISD, where he leads several programs, including beginner accordion classes, drumline, choir, ukulele, and the elementary Conjunto band, LFE Conjunto.

In addition to teaching, Mr. Castillo is a well-known musician, accordionist, and music producer. He arranges and records original music for songwriters from his home studio.

Drawing on years of experience, Mr. Castillo developed this curriculum to guide complete beginners from their first notes to performance readiness. All of the recordings in this book were composed and recorded by Mr. Castillo, who performed every instrumental part himself.

About the Authors
Jesse Bautista

Jesse Bautista holds a Bachelor's degree in Music Education from the University of Texas Rio Grande Valley (2019) and is currently pursuing a Master's degree in Music Education at the same institution.

Jesse teaches elementary music at Los Fresnos CISD in the Rio Grande Valley, located at the southern tip of Texas. He works with PreK - 5th grade students, providing general music education while also leading several after-school programs, including choir, modern band club, and a cover band.

In addition to his work in the classroom, Jesse has a passion for graphic design and was responsible for the layout and graphics featured throughout this book.

Jesse Bautista

Made in the USA
Coppell, TX
04 February 2026

70214935R00046